Marketing and PR

UNCOVERED

Catherine Harris

Marketing & PR Uncovered
This first edition published in 2003 by Trotman and Company Ltd
2 The Green, Richmond, Surrey TW9 1PL

© Trotman and Company Limited 2003

Editorial and Publishing Team

Author Catherine Harris
Editorial Mina Patria, Editorial Director; Rachel Lockhart,
Commissioning Editor; Anya Wilson, Editor; Erin Milliken,
Editorial Assistant.
Production Ken Ruskin, Head of Pre-press and Production
Sales and Marketing Deborah Jones, Head of Sales & Marketing

Designed by XAB

British Library Cataloguing in Publication Data
A catalogue record for this book is available
from the British Library

ISBN 0 85660 896 3

Typeset by Palimpsest Book Production Limited,
Polmont, Stirlingshire

Printed and bound in Great Britain by
Creative Print & Design (Wales) Ltd

CONTENTS

Introduction

WHY READ THIS BOOK?

This book will make you a success and ensure you spend the rest of your days in happiness.

No, sorry, this guide won't do that. It's only a book! But it can help you find a career that suits you, giving you a lot more chance of lifelong success and happiness.

With so many career paths to choose from it's easy to feel panicked. But don't worry. Information is power. So stop, take a deep breath, and read on.

You're doing the first thing right. Research. Finding out as much as you can about a prospective career is the best way to work out if it's for you. Give yourself time: this is an important decision.

Remember, everyone has to start somewhere. Even bigwigs in the marketing and PR world once started with a simple idea that this might be the right sort of career for them.

ASK NOT WHAT YOU CAN DO FOR THE JOB, BUT WHAT THE JOB CAN DO FOR YOU

The information in this book should help crystallise your thinking, tell you what marketing and PR are about and what skills and qualifications you need, and encourage you to think why this work appeals to you and whether it fits in with your personal values and personality type. That second bit is really important.

A job is for life, not just for Christmas. According to the Office of National Statistics, the average person in Britain spends 37.3 hours working every week – that's 1,716 hours a year, assuming you get six weeks holiday annually. Over a career spanning 40 years that's 68,640 hours. Where's all this leading? Simple. You might as well like your job.

It's easy to feel nervous when starting out on a new career. But remember, as a person you have a lot to offer. By getting the right focus, experience and qualifications you can get to where you want to go.

Trotman guides give you the truth about jobs – warts and all. Forget the stereotypes, our guides will help you decide if you're dreaming the right dreams.

Whether you're looking for your first job or a seasoned worker looking for a career change, read on to find out if marketing and PR are really for you.

WHAT'S THE POINT OF MARKETING AND PR?

The bottom line is that marketing and PR are connected to sales. Marketing and PR jobs exist to shift products. Whether you are involved in maintaining a company's good reputation or developing and promoting new products, the point is sustained and increased profitability. Creativity obviously plays a big part, but coming up with exciting ideas is only as good as the sales results they create. Even in the not-for-profit and government sector, selling a message will be the driver. Marketing is now so important to business that it is increasingly common for marketing directors to become CEOs (chief executive officers) of companies. Marketing is all about understanding the market in order to satisfy the changing demands of customers.

WHY BE IN MARKETING AND PR?

Marketing and PR are result-orientated industries and as such are fast moving, exciting and can be extremely creative. For many, increasing the sales or success of an organisation is rewarding. Marketing and PR combine sound business sense with creativity, the opportunity to see your ideas turn into reality and excellent career prospects with good financial rewards. The ultimate rush has to be working on developing a successful new product or a campaign that changes public perceptions. Unfortunately, not all campaigns do that!

CAMPAIGN CRACKERS

- Pepsi – re-branded itself blue and became the drink of a generation

- Blair Witch – do believe the hype

- Guinness – once for the old, now for all.

CAMPAIGN CALAMITIES

- The Millennium Dome – no matter how much money was spent on promotions, it was still the flop of the century. Egg on faces all round.

- When British Airways changed the logos on their planes there was an outcry and they had to be painted back.

- Royal Mail – one of the most famous brands in the UK – made the decision to change its name to Consignia. The name change was declared a failure and now we're back with the good old Royal Mail.

CELEB CASH

If you get the right product with the right star, sales can rocket.

Celebrity endorsement is a big part of the communications business, whether a star is lending their name to a charitable organisation, or a celeb is being paid bucketloads of money to endorse a product.

A high-profile celebrity endorsement deal will be worth around £1 million plus. Nice money if you can get it.

Successful partnerships like David Beckham and Brylcreem or Liz Hurley and Estee Lauder pay out big for businesses and stars.

A match made in heaven
Global megastar Beckham is said to earn around £10 million a year from corporate endorsements with deals from huge companies including Adidas, Vodafone and Marks and Spencer. The Beckham brand is thought to be worth somewhere in the region of £40 million.

Crisptastic
Gary Lineker's association with Walkers has sold an estimated £140 million worth of crisps. The campaign plays on Lineker's 'nice guy' image – the idea being that Walkers crisps taste so good they can turn a saint into a sinner.

HOW MUCH, MATE?
For every £1 spent on the Sainsbury's Jamie Oliver campaign, the return for Sainsbury's was around £37.33. Love those ads or hate them – one thing is undeniable – they work!

Source: T4 Star Bucks

THE TOP THIRTY ADS OF ALL TIME

Channel 4 and *The Sunday Times* recently got together to find out what the nation thinks are the greatest TV ads ever. They discovered that by the age of 35 the average person has watched 150,000 TV ads – the equivalent to two months of your life spent watching commercials on the television. With that in mind, we should all be experts.

The nation's favourites are listed below. But what are yours? Make a list of your top ten and from now on watch ads like a professional. Ask yourself which ads you like, which you don't, and find out what your peer group thinks too. Try to think why certain ads work for you while others don't. Think who the target market is. Excellent: you're already thinking like a top communicator.

1. Guinness – horses and surfers
2. Smash – Martians
3. Tango – orange man
4. Electric Central Heating – creature comforts
5. Boddingtons – Melanie Sykes/ice cream
6. Levi's – launderette/Nick Kamen
7. R. White's – secret lemonade drinker
8. Hamlet – baldy man in photo booth
9. Walkers – Gary Lineker
10. Impulse – acting on . . . first gay ad
11. Cinzano – Leonard Rossiter/Joan Collins
12. Renault Clio – Papa/Nicole
13. Yellow Pages – J. R. Hartley
14. BT – Maureen Lipman/ 'ology'
15. Nike – park life: Eric Cantona, David Seaman, Ian Wright etc.
16. Coca-Cola – teach the world to sing
17. Carling Black Label – dambusters
18. Shake 'n' Vac – dancing woman
19. Andrex – puppies
20. Real coal fires – dog, cat and mouse
21. Ferrero Rocher – ambassador's party
22. Oxo – family/Katie
23. Cornetto – just one Cornetto
24. PG Tips – Mr Shifter
25. Castlemaine – a xxxx one: sherry
26. Flake – girl
27. Milky Bar – Milky Bar Kid
28. Hovis – boy on bike
29. Heineken – refreshes (water in Majorca)
30. Kit Kat – pandas

Source: channel4.co.uk

THERE'S NO SUCH THING AS BAD PUBLICITY

Whether it's an ad that outrages, like the naked image of Sophie Dahl for Opium, an outrageous gaming promotion, or someone caught cheating on a TV show, in some cases bad publicity can increase sales.

Seventeen million viewers tuned in to watch the famous cough 'n' cheat *Who Wants to Be a Millionaire?* programme, in which Major Ingram made his botched fraud attempt. Celador, the show's production company, are said to have made about a million pounds in TV rights from the Major's exploits and gained an enormous amount of free publicity into the bargain. (Source: guardian.co.uk.)

MARKETING AND PR PLAYERS

Who are the gods and goddesses of communications? When these people speak, people listen. They know everything there is to know about marketing, PR or both and are some of the biggest UK players in the field.

- Richard Branson – the king of entrepreneurs and publicity creation

- Rita Clifton – chief executive of Interbrand

- Matthew Freud – mega famous head of Freud Communications

- Max Clifford – publicity man with a finger in many pies; clients have included Michael Barrymore and Simon Cowell.

JARGON BUSTERS	
above the line	advertising in press, TV or other media.
below the line	promotions that are not direct advertisements, such as reduced price offers and premiums.
brainstorm	two heads are better than one. When ideas are scarce get together for a brainstorm.
brief	the outline of what needs to be done on any project.
client	he/she who must be obeyed and sucked up to.
copy	what you call an article when it's being written and before publication (e.g., 'can you e-mail me your copy by 4.00pm?').

demographics	statistics that tell you about society and consumers, e.g., births, deaths and age profiles of populations.
direct marketing	getting the information to individuals, usually done by post, telephone, email or text.
embargo	information in a press release can be embargoed until a certain date. The news will not be published until the date stated on the press release.
FMCG	fast-moving consumer goods. Stuff we eat or use quickly, such as food and drink.
market position	(or market share). Mine's bigger than yours. Finding out who's getting most business in a market by comparing your productivity and success with your competitors.
marks	mistakes are annotated on copy when it is proofread – these annotations are called marks.
pitch	agencies pitch to clients to try and get work. Pitches have to be exciting and well informed and make clients part with their money.
press release	a statement issued by an organisation and sent to the press. Anything from news on a product launch to comment on a business scandal.
selling-in	calling journalists to make sure they have received your press release while trying to persuade them that you're not wasting their time.
strap lines	nothing to do with being whipped! The strap line is the slogan or phrase that appears on an ad (e.g., 'Men can't help acting on Impulse').
trannie	no, not an office transvestite: this is the media industry's name for

transparencies of photographic images used for publication. Currently being superseded by electronic images in gif or j-peg format.

USP   unique selling point: a product's single attribute that makes it a saleable commodity and makes it stand out against its competitors.

THE MARKETING PROFESSIONAL

What do you love about your job?
Working in a young, vibrant company, the trips to Ibiza and all the lovely people I meet. Plus having the freedom to get on with my work and be creative.

What do you hate about it?
The office sound clash and some of the pretentious idiots you come across occasionally.

How did you get into it?
I worked for a couple of marketing agencies in London before applying for the job advertised in the *Guardian*. Easy peasy!

Christine Cowen, 26, Commercial Manager and Head of Marketing at Ministry of Sound, London

THE PR PROFESSIONAL

What do you do?
My role is to develop and implement proactive media relations strategies that will increase the impact of our campaigns, research and policy development. I advise senior staff and commissioners on handling the media, and I have to make sure we are in a position to respond rapidly to news stories about sex equality issues.

What do you love?
The variety – I could be dealing with the *FT* one minute, *Cosmopolitan* the next, and then get a call from the *Engineer* magazine. It's also great to work in a political environment for an organisation working towards goals that I support so strongly myself.

What do you hate?
Filing.

What advice would you give to someone starting out?
Try to get experience in a variety of environments so you can work out what suits you best.

Catherine Evans, 32, Media Manager, Equal Opportunities Commission, London

THE MARKETING MANAGER
What makes you get up in the morning?
I like working on specific projects that are linked to humanitarian issues. We've just done a campaign on how war affects women. Also this year the ICRC organised a big conference bringing together governmental and NGO experts on various issues relating to the problem of people missing in conflict. My department worked on all communication aspects including producing brochures, exhibitions and overseeing video production.

Now we are working on a communication project that deals with children in war, addressing issues such as the reunification of children after war and child soldiers.

What makes you hide under the duvet?
I oversee a team of ten people. Inevitably there is a lot of administration related to that and I find that aspect quite dull. As in most jobs, there are internal politics that waste everybody's time.

What skills are needed for your job?

For my job you need to be able to see the big picture but also have a good eye for detail. Communication skills are extremely important. You need to be able to manage people, co-ordinate projects and think strategically. Although working with numbers is not a big part of my job, it is essential to have a basic understanding of statistics and to be able to manage a budget.

Any tips on giving presentations?

I used to hate giving presentations but I feel much calmer about them now. The more you do them on the same subject the easier they become. My advice would be always prepare well. It doesn't matter if you're nervous, but people will not forgive you if you are ill informed.

How did you get here?

I did a business studies degree, specialised in marketing in Britain and while I was doing that I did internships during the holidays in humanitarian organisations. After university I worked in marketing and advertising in the private sector for a few years. Then I took a career break in my late twenties and did an MA in communications and after that took on a role here. My advertising background is useful when dealing with advertising agencies because I know how their system works. This is particularly helpful as communicating our message can be complex, as we are a strictly independent and neutral organisation. This can make it difficult for agencies to come up with creative ideas that don't conflict with our position.

What advice would you give to someone starting out?

I think, to work in my field, you have to prove that you have a real and sustained commitment to humanitarian issues. Today many people are interested in working for the ICRC. Doing an internship in college holidays is a good idea. Also get some specific communications qualifications and work experience. Organisations like the ICRC are moving towards much more professionalised communications departments.

At the ICRC, it used to be that generalists with field experience were seen as the best people to work in communications but now the ICRC looks more to communications professionals to fill certain specialised posts.

Mohini Ghai, 32, Head of the Marketing and Distribution Unit at the International Committee of the Red Cross (ICRC) in Geneva.

THE PR PROFESSIONAL
What makes you get up in the morning?
I've always been into music. My job is to promote our artists. I've only been doing the job for six months but I've learnt so much already. You couldn't do this job if you didn't love music though. Everyone I've met in the business knows their stuff. I used to DJ at university. I was never that good at it. But it helped me decide what I wanted to do. The greatest thing about my job is feeling like you're in the middle of it all.

Paul Nolan, 28, PR Executive for an international music label, Manchester

CHAPTER 1

The Truth About PR and Marketing

COMMUNICATIONS IN THE UK - THE STATE WE'RE IN

The good news is that the Brits are brilliant at marketing communications and the UK is known as a centre of excellence across the world. As an industry it makes an awful lot of money. The world market in public relations is worth a staggering £10 billion and the UK accounts for around 10% of that, with an industry worth £1 billion.

Even better news if you're thinking of going into PR, the rate of growth in the number of PR jobs over the last fifteen years is higher than any other management function, according to the Institute of Public Relations.

The UK advertising industry has an annual turnover of around £18 billion, while market research alone is worth around £1.5 billion. (Source: Office of National Statistics.)

In 2003 advertising revenues went down as markets reverberated from the effects of September 11 and the Iraq war. Marketing and

PR have been affected by the wider global economic waves but communications and product development are essential when consumer confidence is lower than normal. Peter Fisk, Chief Executive Officer at the Chartered Institute of Marketing (CIM) says: 'Marketing is ultimately about driving business results. Companies that continue to develop their brands efficiently in tough times not only help to sustain profitability in the short-term, but are also much better placed to achieve exceptionally strong results on the upturn. In an economic downturn marketers must defend their budgets by proving that investing in marketing drives long-term business value.'

ADVICE FROM THOSE IN THE KNOW

Why should you go into marketing and PR? As we said in the Introduction, the reasons you choose a particular career are important. If you truly understand your motivation when opting for a particular career, it will make it easier to focus on what you want from a chosen job and to plan how you want your career to develop. We asked some people in the know why marketing and PR could be the career choice for you. This is what they came up with:

FOUR TOP TIPS FROM THE CHARTERED INSTITUTE OF MARKETING (CIM)

- Marketing is one of the most important business activities and therefore a sound career choice.

- Individuals are normally rewarded according to ability rather than age.

- Personal qualities such as interpersonal and communications skills and the ability to work in a team are essential.

- Vital skills for future marketers include management and information technology as well as financial and analytical skills.

FOUR TOP TIPS FROM THE INSTITUTE OF PUBLIC RELATIONS (IPR)

- A career in public relations offers outstanding opportunities to work in a fast-moving, varied, creative and people-orientated environment.

- It can be extremely rewarding – PR is a serious strategic business function and you'll be able to see the positive outcomes of your work, and how you are making a difference to organisational success.

- For those with the talent and motivation, the opportunities for career development are excellent.

- PR is a flexible profession and, with the right skills and knowledge, you'll be able to move up the career ladder and to move between different sectors and working environments.

MARKETING AND PR – THE NUMBERS

With marketing and PR making all those billions for the British economy, it's no surprise that there are loads of people working in marketing and PR in Britain.

PR

- There are over 48,000 people working in PR in the UK, according to the Institute of Public Relations (IPR).

- Just over half (56%) work in house.

- Just under half (44%) work in consultancies – anything from a huge international agency to a one-man freelance.

- The biggest PR employer is the Government Information Service.

Source: connexionsonline government careers advice.

MARKETING

- The Chartered Institute of Marketing (the largest marketing body in the UK) currently has 40,000 UK members.

- 30,000 of them are studying for CIM qualifications.

WONGA IN YOUR WALLET

At entry level, salaries in marketing and PR are likely to be somewhere between £10,000 and £23,000. The average marketing trainee based in London will probably be on somewhere around £17,000 and £18,000 a year. Most London salaries are a bit higher than in the rest of the UK because of the expense of living in the capital.

PR CASH
(Average salaries)

In house	Private	Public
PR Officer	£21,600	£21,500
PR Manager	£34,200	£28,800
Head of Communications	£51,300	£38,000

Consultancy	
Account Executive	£20,000
Account Manager	£25,600
Account Director	£37,200
Board Director	£51,000
Chairman/MD	£61,500

Freelance	£43,600

Figures from Institute of Public Relations 2003

MARKETING CASH

Marketing Clerk	£13,000–£15,000
Marketing Assistant	£17,400–£20,000
Marketing Officer	£20,500–£25,000
Marketing Executive	£27,000–£32,000
Product Manager	£28,000–£36,000
Advertising Manager	£52,000+
Brand Manager	£47,000+

Marketing Manager   £44,000–£62,000
Marketing Director   £56,000–£100,000+
Figures from CIM, 2001

CHANGES IN COMMUNICATIONS

As a nation, in 2001 we spent an estimated £20 billion on branded fashion goods alone. Brands are big business and marketing and PR professionals have to work hard to keep their brand one step ahead of the rest. One of the ways they can do this is to keep up to date with the rapid technological changes that allow them to target consumers in new and ingenious ways.

Technological changes like the Internet and mobile phones have created a more personalised means of communications for advertisers. Communications can now reach individuals anywhere. The global reach of communications is clearly expressed when you realise that audio blogs were recently transmitted to a website from mountain climbers scaling Everest.

Better and more sophisticated means of communication also mean that it is easier for companies to collect data on all sorts of individual preferences. This has created a new trend in advertising, moving towards a personalised advertising message as well as a group message.

Alongside more traditional methods like TV advertising, many campaigns now use wide-reaching methods like viral marketing as part of the campaign. Think about how you communicate – picture messaging, SMS, and email – these are all means by which companies increasingly look to promote products.

THE FAT LADY HAS HER LAST FAG
It's not just changes in technology that marketers, PR people and advertisers have to keep up with. Changes in the law have a big impact on the communications business. In February 2003 the government banned tobacco advertising. Silk Cut marked the occasion with the Fat Lady Singing campaign – an opera singer in a purple silk dress sings with

her arms open while her dress has split, forming a single 'silk cut'. Everyone knows the advertisers will find new ways round the ban. The restrictions on cigarette advertising in the past have led to some of the most creative ads of all time. The concept for the Benson and Hedges series has always been seen as a design classic. Look out to see what they come up with next.

HOW WE COMMUNICATE WITH EACH OTHER
Recent developments in technology, like the Internet, have changed the way people receive news.

In Europe alone there are around 171 million people online, according to public affairs consultancy Apco.

There are 11.4 million homes online in the UK (source: ONS).

The Internet is big business and communicators have to understand it thoroughly to make sure they are making the most of its potential.

In the UK we send 1 billion texts messages per month (source: www.bbc.co.uk).

Non-terrestrial TV networks are becoming increasingly popular in the UK. In April 2003, for the first time the combined viewers of non-terrestrial TV outweighed the audience numbers of the five main terrestrial stations.

POP UPS? POP OFF!
Don't you just hate those annoying pop ups that make your computer go even slower? But guess what? They work. A 2003 study by the European Interactive Advertising Association discovered that online ads extend a brand's

reach by about 10% and increase the public's knowledge of the brand by about 6%.

Interestingly, online advertising has been nowhere near as successful as it was expected to be in the heady days of late nineties dotcomania. However, in the recent ad slump it is one of the growth sectors. The amount spent by advertisers on the web has grown by 19% year on year to £196.7m in 2002, according to figures from PricewaterhouseCoopers released in April 2003.

DOES MY BRAND LOOK BIG IN THIS?

Clever professional communicators are constantly thinking of new ways to get people talking about their brand or organisation. Forget bus shelters and billboards: did you know that people and animals are the new advertising spaces?

GETTING AHEAD IN ADVERTISING

A man in America has taken the idea of being a human billboard so far that he has actually had a brand name tattooed onto the back of his shaved head. By contract the tattoo must stay visible for five years. David Beckham famously has the names of his children Brooklyn and Romeo tattooed on his body: but will sponsors be asking for more from their celebrity endorsers in the future?

Students in the UK are lining up to brand themselves for money. With student debts piling up, what could be more appealing than £88.20 a week to wear a corporate logo on your forehead for a measly three hours a day? The logos or messages are applied in vegetable dye. But studious studos should beware. The advertising must be done when students are out and about, the burying of heads in books just doesn't count! The national campaign, linked with FHM and 'yoof' channel CNX, was thought up by agency 'Cunning Stunts' – the same people who projected Gail Porter's now famous naked rear on to the Houses of Parliament. Go to www.cunningstunts.net to see some really creative ideas.

Cunning Stunts calls itself the first ambient and guerilla marketing agency in the UK. Ambient marketing – non-traditional marketing – grew by 400% in 2002 (source: *Campaign*).

JUST CALL ME PEPSI

In 2002, over 6,000 people in the UK responded to a request from British games company UK Acclaim to turn themselves into human billboards. Candidates had to be willing to change their name for one year to Turok, a character from Acclaim UK's latest game who just happened to be a Native American with a penchant for slaying dragons. This kind of marketing – identity marketing – shows the kind of imagination needed to be at the forefront of communications. Incredibly, the financial incentive for the name-changers was quite small. To be a living billboard for a year the reward was an Xbox Console and £500. So what's the future? People calling their newborn babies Pepsi or Nike? We'll have to wait and see. But it doesn't sound impossible. Come to think of it, a Pepsi or a Nike would fit right in with Chardonnay in TV's *Footballer's Wives*.

WHAT YOU SAY, DAWG?

There's no such thing as just walking the dog any more. Mega businesses like Sony Ericsson are wising up to dogverts. In December 2002 the mobile phone company used big dogs as walking, wagging billboards to promote their new photo message service. Dogs in cities across the UK were walked wearing dog coats sporting logo and strap line. Dogverts are the brainchild of Dutch company Dogvertising. The thinking is, if it moves and people see it, advertise on it. What could be next? Jogverts, pramverts, traffic wardenverts, bus conductorverts. The list is endless.

WHO SAID THAT?

A Scottish design company has come up with the novel idea of talking billboards. Infra-red sensors located at the back of the billboard can detect when someone is passing by and start a recorded message or sound. A drink could be heard to pour, a cereal could be crunched or a celebrity could be heard to speak. A possible problem is noise pollution, but the future for this device is exciting. Imagine a poster inviting you to take a holiday in Barbados with the sound of the sea hitting the shores. What's next? Billboards that smell? With the general trend towards more individualised marketing, could billboards talk to us personally in the future? Whichever way it goes, you can be sure that some clever marketing or PR person will be thinking up new ways to promote their product. It might be you who comes up with the next big idea.

THINKING LATERALLY

Creative promotions don't just have to be about new technology. A good idea can be as simple as putting two things together that no one has thought of before. In the spring of 2003 the government and London's black cabbies launched a campaign against domestic violence. All black cab drivers now carry information on where to get help for domestic violence and are given an awareness-raising talk. Over 300 cabs were commissioned to carry the logo 'Domestic violence – together we can put an end to it'. The launch of the campaign generated widespread media interest and was a clever, cheap idea. One in four people in London use a taxi at least once a month and there are almost two million taxi trips a week. It is estimated that the campaign will reach around 26,000 cab drivers. Barbara Roche, Minister for Social Exclusion and Equality, said this about the campaign:

'I believe this imaginative campaign will help to provide women at risk and their families with crucial information when they need it most. Leaving home is a last resort, it may involve children and it may come after a long period abuse.

'By the nature of their job, cab drivers may encounter women at risk. We're not asking them to become counsellors, but by using special taxi receipts or driving them to the nearest hospital or police station, they could be helping someone into a safer future.

'Research suggests that providing information to women experiencing domestic violence on where and how to access help needs to be approached creatively. We need to weave it into their everyday lives.'

Communications don't just have to be about products. You can change the way people think and make lives better.

MARKETING AND THE INTERNET
How many visitors do you get?
Monthly we get over 4 million page impressions

How many are there in your team?
Three.

How did you get your job?
I was headhunted from my CV on the net.

What do you love about it?
I have never been bothered about the type of website I work on, it is the functionality and people that make it enjoyable. Foxton's aims to be the best London property website there is and I think the award (British Interactive Media Association's Grand Prix Award and Public Services Award) proves we achieve that. The exciting thing is we are continuously trying to make it better! The web team also works on many of the internal systems at Foxton's, which allows us to meet different types of challenges.

What drives you mad?
There's never enough time to do everything you would like to, but I'd rather that than be bored!

What's the growth area in marketing for estate agents?
The web has been the most significant development for estate agents over the last few years and I see it continuing to make a big impact and we continue to explore other avenues such as SMS, e-mail and any other avenues available.

Leo Lapworth, 28, Senior Web Developer for Foxton's Estate Agents, London

E-BUSINESS IS BIG BUSINESS

Tesco's e-commerce site made £447 million in online sales in 2002, up 26% on 2001. This led to a thirty-fold increase in profits from £400,000 to £12.2 million.

Tesco's web shopping site processes around 110,000 weekly orders. Tesco.com has a reach that covers about 95% of the population. (Source: Ukonline for business.)

So e-business is big business. The Internet is not only a great tool for businesses to market their goods, and for research and promotion, it's also a point of sale for their customers. UK Online for Business offers the following advice to small businesses on marketing on the Internet.

Market research

The Internet is great for market research. Look at competitors' websites and use the Internet as a tool for customer surveys, business reports, specialist data, and market analysis.

Promotion

The Internet is a fantastic tool for promotion. You don't need to waste time on mailshots trying to drum up new business: customers can find out about services and products via the website.

Directing customers to the site

Getting in a good position on a search engine is vital. You need to optimise key words on the site and ask other websites to link through to your site – hyperlinks boost search ratings. The surest way of controlling a position on a search engine is by paying.

Attracting and keeping new customers

The key is to keep them interested and get their details. By getting them to register for special offers you have a means of communication with your e-customers.

Market to existing customers
Don't forget to stay focused on your existing customers. A website can offer them instant home access to products and services.

GROWTH AREAS
The Internet and information systems are the future in marketing – that's the latest from the Chartered Institute of Marketing (CIM) Marketing Trends Survey.

Keep your eyes on telecommunications and corporate social responsibility (CSR) – that's a hot tip from the Institute of Public Relations (IPR).

CORPORATE SOCIAL RESPONSIBILITY (CSR)
Corporations play such a large role in our society that increasingly they are being held to account. More and more organisations must find a way to give back to the community to be perceived as credible organisations. Recent research from the Institute of Business Ethics suggests that companies who are committed to ethical behaviour make more money in the long run than companies who are less committed.

It is a difficult area to record accurately – ethical business is to some extent a subjective concept. The Institute of Business Ethics at www.ibe.org.uk is a good place to find out more.

Consumers are more and more interested in how a company's goods have been made. The combination of consumer interest in a company's ethics and the fact that more ethical business behaviour appears to be improving the bottom line is bound to further increase growth in the area of corporate social responsibility.

The communication of issues related to corporate social responsibility is an extremely delicate area. While multinational companies look for ways to improve the communities in which they do business, by sponsoring schemes related to everything from homelessness to education, sometimes this corporate philanthropy can be perceived to be purely cynical.

When chocolate giant Cadbury launched their £9 million UK campaign Cadbury Get Active in 2003 the company was slated by the press for encouraging kids to eat more chocolate in the guise of encouraging them to live healthier lives. In fact the scheme had won the support of the government and a sports charity. Kids could earn sports equipments for their schools by collecting chocolate tokens. Journalists started to do the maths. The *Guardian* reported, 'A set of posts and net for volleyball for secondary schoolchildren would require, for example, tokens from 5,440 chocolate bars.' Cadbury's countered that this was an initiative to combat obesity, a condition related to sedentary lifestyles, and that they didn't imagine only children would collect the tokens, but family and friends as well – much like the Computers for Schools campaigns run by a major supermarket.

The Cadbury example highlights the problems of corporate social responsibility. It is a fascinating area, and as companies wise up to their new role in the wider community more and more such schemes will be implemented. The challenge will be to create credible schemes that have a real positive effect and generate positive publicity for the organisation.

WHO YOU WORK FOR

Are you happy to work for a global conglomerate? There are arguments for and against globalisation. Because marketing and PR are used for everything from consumer goods to government policy, you need to be aware of what you are getting involved in. Don't walk into a job with your eyes closed. If you want to know more about how big western business can mess up people's lives in the developing world, visit Oxfam's website at www.oxfam.org.uk and read about Fair Trade. To discover more about environmentally friendly jobs go to www.peopleandplanet.org.uk.

ARE PR AND MARKETING FOR YOU?

So you think you know everything there is to know about PR and marketing? It's not all knocking back the Bolly with Matthew Freud and Meg Matthews or bouncing brand ideas off Trevor Beattie, you know. Try our quiz to find out if your dreams are anything like the reality.

PR QUIZ

1.   You are exhausted and just about to finish off on Friday at 5.00pm. All you want to do is get to the pub. A journalist from a national Sunday newspaper calls up and asks you for a long list of urgent information and isn't that polite about it either.

     Do you:
     a) say you'll find out for them and then not call them back. You've got a date and work isn't going to take over your life.
     b) take the time to let them know what information you can get them by their deadline and make sure you get if for them. You're tired but this is an important contact.
     c) tell them to bog off. They should have called earlier and it's not your fault they are stressed.

2.   Everyone on your team is getting together for a brainstorm to think up some ideas for a new product launch.

Do you:
a) think it's fun to come up with ideas and enjoy sparking off other people's suggestions.
b) sit quietly and get fed up listening to idiots who love the sound of their own voices.
c) not go as you're late writing a press release and you can't find the time.

3. **You work in a freelance agency. You're about to give a pitch to a big new client and it's important to the agency that you win the business. The pressure is on.**

   Do you:
   a) take a taxi straight to the airport – there's no way you're going to get up in front of those people.
   b) wing it. You know your stuff and you're a bit of talker.
   c) prepare for it thoroughly – it's a bit daunting but you'll feel great once you've done it.

4. **You're at a celebrity launch and are in charge of co-ordinating media interviews.**

   Do you:
   a) forget what you're doing, you're too busy chatting up the celebrities.
   b) make sure you fit in as many media interviews as possible and keep an eye on the celebrities to ensure they keep endorsing your product/organisation.
   c) feel too embarrassed to talk to anyone and stand quietly in the corner.

5. **You've got a deadline for a press release, media enquiries stacking up and your boss has just bawled you out because the MD of your company has sent out a memo complaining about some negative coverage.**

   Do you:
   a) burst into tears and book yourself in for therapy.

b) feel under pressure but realise it's just one of those days and keep working.

c) send a rude e-mail to the MD saying she should have a go at your job. You'd like to see her do any better.

ANSWERS

1. The right answer is b). There will be times when you will be dying to go home, but some contacts are just too important. You need to be reliable and able to work out how to prioritise.

2. The right answer is a). You don't have to be the next Leonardo da Vinci to work in PR, but enjoying ideas and creativity does help. You will also have to juggle new projects and existing ones, and will have to prioritise your work effectively.

3. The right answer is b). There is usually an element of public speaking in PR, whether it's pitching ideas, introducing launches and press conferences or briefing people. Don't panic if you're not a brilliant public speaker, as experience does help and you can get training. Go the IPR website (see Chapter 6) for more information.

4. The right answer is b). It is likely that at some point in your PR career you will have to co-ordinate media interviews, whether it is with a representative from an organisation, or a celebrity endorsing a project or product. You do need to be outgoing, sociable and not too starstruck. No matter how fun a launch may seem, you've got to keep your focus on why the launch is happening.

5. The right answer is b). PR does get really stressful. If you get a buzz from a fast-paced environment then that level of stress is likely to suit you. You can't be over-sensitive: you are occasionally going to get caught in the crossfire. If that happens you still have to get your work done. Diplomacy is also a large part of PR. If you are a hothead, it's probably not the career for you.

MARKETING QUIZ

1. You are about to give a presentation to explain how a recent marketing initiative has increased sales and improved profitability.

   Do you:
   a) pull a sickie because you can't make the figures add up and you hate thinking in numbers.
   b) not bother with the figures – what they want to hear about is the campaign.
   c) look forward to letting everyone know about the figures. You've done the number crunching and the results are excellent.

2. Your senior boss, the brand manager, has asked you to come up with a new marketing initiative for an existing product.

   Do you:
   a) panic and make something up – you don't know anything about theory.
   b) work out a strategy to use a new marketing theory that you've been reading about.
   c) how are you supposed to think up a new initiative? They don't pay you enough to do that.

3. You are watching your favourite TV programme and there's an ad break.

   Do you:
   a) switch over to the other side – the sickening cancer of consumerism in our society makes you angry.
   b) go and make a cup of tea – ads bore you.
   c) watch avidly to understand which ads work well and why.

4. Your company is just about to launch a new product. The campaign preparations are going well. At the eleventh hour

your boss gives you the copy of an ad that will be going into print. He wants you to review and edit it before he has a look at it.

Do you:
a) go to the toilet and hide. You hate responsibility of any kind.
b) sit down and start work: you want everything to be perfect.
c) wish you had more time: you hate doing things under pressure.

5. **You are managing a range of suppliers and agencies and need to make sure a whole load of projects get finished on time.**

    Do you:
    a) rely on the suppliers to meet their deadlines – after all, that is what they are paid for.
    b) work out a project management schedule and keep to it closely. Keep on top of the suppliers.
    c) get someone else to do it. You got into marketing to be creative.

ANSWERS

1. The right answer is c). All aspects of marketing require you to be numerate, whether you're dealing with budgets or working with market research. If the thought of working with numbers makes you feel sick, marketing may not be the career for you.

2. The right answer is b). The business environment and marketing theories are constantly evolving. You need to keep up to date with current trends. You also need to be able to think strategically and be able to convey your thinking clearly to others working in your team.

3. The right answer is c). You'll need an interest in ads and consumer trends to enjoy marketing.

4. The right answer is b). You will need to be flexible, adaptable under pressure and be able to take all kinds of responsibility even when you are at a junior level.

5. The right answer is b). Management skills become increasingly important in marketing as you rise up the career ladder. However, even at junior level you can be expected to manage projects.

IS THE JOB RIGHT FOR YOU?

MARKETING

The core competencies that every marketer needs are:

● planning

● marketing strategy

● process management

● managing agencies

● project management

● financial management.

Also useful:

● creativity

● innovation

● leadership skills

● self management

● time management

● presentation skills.

Want to get inside the head of a brilliant marketer? David Wright, head of corporate marketing at the Chartered Institute of Marketing, says it's all about asking the right questions. 'If the organisation didn't exist, would there be a customer need to invent or establish it?' If not, the organisation needs to find a point of differentiation from the competition.

Recent research, commissioned by the Chartered Institute of Marketing, shows that at an operational level, marketers need to know what their organisation's marketing objectives are for the year in terms of brand share, return on investment and customer loyalty. Each organisation should ask:

● What is your current market and brand share?

● What are the marketing programmes for the year, and how do they tie in with your organisation's marketing objectives?

● Who are your key competitors and what are their programmes for the year?

Marketers may not know the answers to all these questions instantly, but if they are not asking the questions in the first place, then they are off the pace.

Marketers can get this information, David Wright says, by talking to customer-facing people in their own organisation, and by picking up on the news and rumours circulating in the distribution channels. Finally, marketers should know how much marketing spend, and through what media, it takes to create a 1% gain in market share.

Today's marketers not only need to respond to and address market volatility, identifying and seeking the best market options for the business, they need an agile mind that can think strategically and innovatively.

PR

Those lovely people at Cranfield School of Management and the Institute of Public Relations (IPR) have got together to work out the skills that are most important to be a PR ace. And this is what they say:

The core competencies that you need to excel at PR are:

● common sense

● energy

● curiosity

● open-mindedness

● flexibility

● creativity

● stamina

● organisation skills

● excellent literacy skills.

During your career you will need to:

● analyse management needs

● advise management

● identify causes of problems, analyse future trends and predict their consequences

● research public opinion, attitudes and expectations, and advise on necessary action

● plan, organise and co-ordinate tasks

● monitor and follow up

● set goals and objectives

- motivate and influence others

- work effectively with journalists

- communicate effectively with individuals and groups in meetings and through presentations

- establish financial controls

- write and edit press releases and reports

- identify major social issues affecting organisations and resolve conflict

- work well with others

- gain project management skills – and have the ability to carry out several different tasks at a given time. PR practitioners have to work within allocated budgets and deadlines

- keep up an ongoing interest in current affairs, especially in the socio-political and economic developments that impact on business

- gain a sound knowledge of the industry sector you work in to help you to operate intelligently. For example, if you work in city and financial PR, you should have a good working knowledge of financial markets, policies and law.

WHAT WILL THE HOURS BE LIKE?
You won't always have to work outside nine to five, but if there is an important pitch, launch or event, you will have to put in the extra hours. This can easily mean 60-hour weeks when you're up against it. In-house work can be less busy as you only have one client – the organisation for which you are working. However, in an agency you are likely to be working on several accounts, all equally important.

PR and marketing will entail work intruding into your free time. In many PR jobs you will be expected to go to launches and functions in the evenings, and you will be working. It's not just guzzling cocktails at a party and mingling with celebrities; more often than not it will be talking shop to business people in suits. Don't go into marketing and PR if you want a nine-to-five job. The work is highly competitive and you will be expected to show enthusiasm – even after hours!

WORKING FREELANCE

LOVE IT

More people than ever before are choosing to go freelance. There is a lot of scope for this in marketing and communications. Freelancers will often be brought in for specific projects. Many companies have a policy of using freelancers because it means they can save on pension contributions and National Insurance, holiday pay and all the other expenses of full-time staff. The following are some of the upsides of freelance.

- you decide when you take your holidays

- variety – the ability to work on lots of different projects for different companies

- being your own boss

- no office politics

- when you're busy, you can make good money.

HATE IT

Those who do choose to go freelance no longer have the safety net of a permanent position. That means they have to constantly pitch work and they don't know where the next pay packet is coming from. These are some of the downsides:

- insecurity – will I be able to pay the mortgage next month?

- projects never end – when you're working for more than one client it can be difficult to stop the projects from running into one another

- expensive overheads – funding your own office space and costs can be crippling financially

- working too hard – most people think that when they work for themselves they will work less hard. The opposite is usually true, as many people become worried about where their next money is coming from and end up taking too much work.

HOW LONG WILL IT TAKE ME TO GET TO THE TOP?
Marketing and PR are notoriously youth-orientated and young people can get to the top quickly. It is normal to see people in their mid- to late-thirties in extremely senior positions. So what happens when you get older? Does everyone over forty lose their job? No. It is a myth that only young people work in marketing and PR. Long-term opportunities with excellent remuneration are available. The route from marketing director to CEO is becoming an established one. However, the pace of the job and the long hours do encourage some people to make a career change towards the end of their careers in PR.

CHAPTER 2

How do Marketing and PR Fit Together?

Many marketing and PR functions are distinct. For example, a PR department will handle all media enquiries and a marketing department will undertake any research into a new product.

The main crossover areas are in promotion, particularly in the area of marketing promotion and proactive PR. (Proactive PR is the opposite of reactive PR: it's when a public relations department sets out to get coverage for the brand or a new product by creating stories for the media.) Marketing promotions will usually include advertising space that is paid for, while PR often generates free media coverage through comment in the press. Both are dedicated to the company's bottom line.

The degree of crossover in promotions means that some positions in communications are available to specialists in both marketing and PR, particularly in smaller companies, where the marketing and PR departments may be rolled into one.

In some larger organisations marketing and PR departments are separate. In cases where internal communications are poor, this can lead to a situation where the left hand doesn't know what the right hand is doing.

Sometimes marketing and PR are under a single senior figure called something like the Director of Communications.

Marketing departments:

● research the market – what do customers want?

● develop the product – listen to the customers and make it so

● price the product – the price is right if sales targets, market place and production and promotion costs are taken into account

● sell the product – but how many do you need? Use sales figures and forecast promotion success rate

● promote the product – work out strategy and oversee relationships with outside agencies such as advertisers

● manage the brand – keep corporate identity on the right track

● after sales analysis – see if campaign sold product effectively

● IN ORDER TO DRIVE SALES.

Public relations departments:

● deal with journalists, send out press releases and respond to inquiries

● generate positive coverage in press for new products and brand image

● manage and plan for crises to minimise negative press coverage

● communicate financial issues to investors

- organise internal communications (possibly an intranet)

- deal with government related issues (public affairs)

- deal with issues of corporate social responsibility

- organise events – to gain media coverage

- IN ORDER TO MAINTAIN REPUTATION AND DRIVE SALES.

HOW DO MARKETING AND PR PROMOTIONS DIFFER?

Despite the areas of crossover in promotions there are often different areas of responsibility.

For example, if a company were to launch a new financial service through digital TV, the marketing department would organise all the advertising (likely to be an integrated campaign across broadcast and print media and the Internet), while the PR department would ensure the media covered the new financial service with positive editorial comment. The key to the main difference between the promotional remit of marketing and PR is that marketing departments oversee advertising and marketing promotions while PR departments usually generate editorial comment.

In our example of the new financial service on digital TV the PR department might initially hold a press conference and provide a good story for specialist financial journalists in the trade, local and national press. They might invite a big star to endorse the product (possibly someone who is already involved with the brand via advertising and the marketing department). The PR department may do a deal with a newspaper to offer their readers 30 free digital televisions as part of their promotions.

As you can see, the PR and marketing message needs to be homogenous for a brand or new product to be successful. PR and marketing support each other as business functions and there is a great deal of crossover. In many cases a PR agency will offer marketing as part of its service and a marketing agency will also offer PR.

WARMING UP THE PRESS FOR A COLD CHALLENGE

Mary Nicholson is co-creator and Head of Marketing and PR for Polar Travel, the extraordinary UK company that takes expeditions of 'ordinary people' to the Arctic and the Antarctic. Mary is an expert in PR and marketing and is essential to the expeditions; she generates the publicity and finds the sponsors to help pay for the expeditions. Without her, they just wouldn't happen.

This extract is taken from her book *Snow Way*. It shows that when it comes to generating publicity, no matter how much work you put in, you don't always get the results you want first time round. Tenacity is what creates results.

In this extract after a tough selection process the names of Polar Travel's first all-women's polar relay team are about to be announced, Mary is having to work hard to find sponsors and is trying to get as much coverage as possible to generate the press interest that will attract them.

'The next day we sent out our final press release to announce The Team. The Press Association came to Kelly College to take details and a picture, and the *Daily Express* was there too. Meanwhile, from my office I had been frantically faxing the rest of the news desks with the following:

"BRITAIN'S TWENTY TOUGHEST WOMEN SELECTED

"The squad of the first ever all women's expedition to the North Pole was selected today, after a hellish SAS-style four day 'yomp' over tors, through bogs and across the rivers of windswept Dartmoor, with virtually no sleep allowed, and no shelter provided.

"Participants were being judged on mental attitude as well as fitness, to ensure that the chosen team will remain positive and calm through extreme physical hardship, including breaking ice, polar bear attacks, and temperatures of -50°C.

"Of the 45 hopefuls who began the weekend, 41 completed the course, with two twisted ankles, 'flu, and exhaustion accounting for those dropping out. Bernie Rochford from Bollington, Cheshire, who did not make the squad, said, 'It was fairly clear who the final team would be after the first day and a half, but I still feel very proud of what I have achieved. I would not have missed this nightmare test for anything . . .'"

'I used my Samsung 500 fax-phone to send out this mailing. I don't think it was designed for multiple mailings of 100 faxes at a time, but it's kept going for eight years.

'After my faxing I raced the twelve miles to Kelly and screamed at the ever-loyal Mike and Julia to hare home and man the phones for the explosion of media interest my faxes would generate. Between them they handled a call from the *Cambridge Evening News* that day. It was a Sunday. The next day, thankfully, the phone was on melt-down.'

The good news is that with Mary's hard work the expedition was a massive success. She eventually got the final sponsorship deal through when McVitie's Penguin biscuits came to the rescue and the expedition became known as the 'McVitie's Penguin Polar Relay'. The women were given Penguins as part of their rations and Penguin biscuits gained excellent branding.

Source: *Snow Way*, Mary Nicholson (quoted with the author's permission)

CHAPTER 3

What You Could Be in Marketing

THE MARKETING MIX

MARKET RESEARCH – THE MARKET RESEARCHER

The point of market research is to find out what customers want. Market researchers use a variety of methods to help companies understand the market place and the customer. Market research is a vital part of any marketing strategy.

PRODUCT DEVELOPMENT – THE DESIGN AND PRODUCTION TEAMS

The challenge for marketers is constantly to come up with new ideas to keep their products fresh and relevant for consumers whose needs and desires change in relation to everything from technological advances to fashion. Product development is a fascinating area. Design and production teams working on anything from cars to trainers react to market research and develop improved and new products. It could be you who designs the next BMW series, the latest surf gear or a new margarine container.

PRICING – THE MARKETING MANAGER AND TEAM

Another key factor in marketing is getting the price right. This is a science: price is determined by juggling sales targets, research from the marketplace, and production and promotion costs. This is usually done by the marketing manager, who has to be a really good strategic thinker to get the price right. Sales results will tell you immediately if you've got it too low or high. Psychology comes into play as well. If you are dealing with luxury goods, for example, consumers sometimes have more confidence in a brand if they spend more money on it. Think of that the next time you're considering that ridiculously expensive item from Gucci.

SALES AND DISTRIBUTION – THE MARKETING MANAGER AND TEAM

Sales and distribution are all about making sure customers have access to the goods so that they can buy them. Much like pricing, getting the demand right is a strategic science. Using sales figures, the marketing manager will have to forecast the level of increased demand as a result of promotions in order to decide how many items are needed. Get this wrong and it's a costly mistake.

PROMOTION – THE MARKETING MANAGER AND TEAM

Strategy is key to promotion. The marketing manager will work out a strategy for product promotion. This is usually where external bodies such as advertising and PR agencies come in. An integrated strategy will be developed with external agencies. Strategies for each country may need to be slightly different – nuances in ad campaigns can have different meanings or no meaning at all in another country.

GETTING LOST IN TRANSLATION
Language can get in the way in international marketing. That great product name may be just the thing for one country but it might be a real stinker elsewhere.

- Japan's Krappy toilet paper wouldn't travel well

- Philippines' sportswear label, the Athlete's Foot, doesn't give quite the right impression.

I'VE GOTTA HAVE IT

Brilliant marketing means everyone is talking about something and dying to spend their money on it.

Marketing requires a mixture of imagination, statistical analysis, strategic thinking and understanding of how and why people buy things. At best it is creative, well paid and challenging. At worst it's stressful, demanding and requires long hours.

A lot of people want to do it. So you have to get ahead of the pack.

But don't be put off! Determination gets you everywhere. If you decide this career is for you there are always ways to break in.

CRM
Customer relationship management (CRM) is the new buzzword in marketing. Rather than treating all customers as equals, CRM focuses on the best customers. Where traditional marketing is product-driven, CRM is customer- driven. So instead of simply finding ways to entice new customers, CRM tries to work out what existing (especially the best) customers want. The Chartered Institute of Marketing (CIM) runs a course in CRM.

THE POWER OF SEVEN

They say three is a magic number, but did you know seven is a marketing magic number? Have you ever heard of the seven Ps of marketing? No? Well, you have now.

- Product

- Packaging

- Position

- Promote at the right Price to the right People to make a Profit.

So marketing people use research to find out what people really want from a business or organisation. They also promote their stuff to a target audience in the way that is most likely to get them to cough up their hard-earned cash. A marketer would be involved in anything from choosing a price to deciding where and how to launch a product.

WE GO TOGETHER

Sponsorship of long-running events is a fantastic way of gaining brand exposure. Some partnerships have become so ingrained in the public mind that you can hardly say one without the other. Think of the Barclaycard Premiership, the Amstel Champions' League, the Flora London Marathon and the BUPA Great North Run. Companies pay buckets of money to be associated with these sporting events and in return gain high-profile coverage every time the event gets media coverage. In many cases there is a specific fit, as with Flora and BUPA and the runs. Both organisations deal in health products, one in low-cholesterol margarine, the other in health insurance and hospitals. By associating themselves with fitness-related events that ordinary people and sports stars participate in, the brands are associated with healthy living.

Marketing professionals need to make the most of sponsorship opportunities and have to be creative, not only to think of where a good fit would be made, but also to make sure the exposure is consistent and positive.

WHERE YOU COULD WORK

Once you start on your marketing career, you can decide whether to work in house or in an agency. Marketing is now recognised as such an important part of business that most companies have their own in-house marketing department. But there are specialist marketing agencies that sell their services on a freelance basis.

WHAT YOU COULD WORK IN – MARKETING SECTORS

- consumer durables – things that last, such as furniture, cookers, TVs

- FMCG (fast-moving consumer goods) – things that don't last, like food and detergents

- services marketing – services we use, e.g. insurance, accounting, legal services, travel services

- industrial (business to business) marketing – anything one business might market to another, such as raw materials, machinery or office furniture

- export marketing – stuff other countries use

- public sector marketing – stuff we need to hear about from the non-commercial sector (e.g. government policy, state benefits or charities).

JOB DESCRIPTIONS

THE MARKETING MANAGER

The marketing manager will oversee the many different aspects of the marketing mix. He or she will work with new and existing products and brand image and the communications strategy to ensure consistent and increased sales. The marketing manager will have to liase with his or her own team and with external organisations such as advertising agencies.

Good marketing managers are:

● excellent communicators (both orally and in writing)

● deadline-focused

● good organisers

● detail-focused

● team players

● good leaders

● good at maths

● good at analysis.

THE MARKET RESEARCH EXECUTIVE

A market research executive collects information to find out what customers want from a business or organisation. Getting the survey right is key to getting the correct information about potential and existing customers. Devising a research strategy based on cost and information needed by the client, a market research executive will also analyse the findings and provide the client with results. Surveys may be for commercial or non-commercial organisations.

A market research executive may work in an agency. He or she will generally work mainly in an office, except when overseeing fieldwork. However, a specialist qualitative research specialist is likely to be far more involved in fieldwork.

MARKET RESEARCH AREAS

CONSUMER RESEARCH
Market research executives working in this field will research public opinion on goods and services sold to the public. Research for the consumer market could be anything from how people choose their breakfast cereal to what makes them join a gym.

INDUSTRIAL OR BUSINESS TO BUSINESS RESEARCH
This is a much more technical area as it deals with specific goods and services used by businesses. Research in the area of business to business marketing could be anything from finding out about the efficiency of a piece of machinery to trying to understand how technological change is affecting an industry's development.

SOCIAL AND POLITICAL RESEARCH
A market research executive working in the social and political field will research public opinion on areas like government policy or administration. Research into social issues could deal with a range of issues – anything from asylum seekers to unemployment.

MARKET RESEARCH – BUZZWORDS

Quantitative research
A large survey of lots of people probably by phone, post, Internet and face to face. Uses fixed questions and data compiled and analysed on computers.

Qualitative research
A small survey conducted with a sample of people, for example a focus group. During a qualitative survey the sample group are more likely to discuss a range of issues than answer specific questions. An in-depth written report is produced for the client when the survey is complete.

THE MARKET RESEARCH INTERVIEWER
All market research requires direct interaction with the customer. This might be on the phone or face to face on the street. If you want this job you'd better like standing on your feet, possibly in the cold and rain.

MARKET RESEARCH – THE MARKETPLACE
There are 2,000 research agencies in London, and the Market Research Society has over 8,000 members. Most agencies are in London and there are only about 250 jobs a year at entry level for recent graduates.

Starting salaries are in the region of £15,000 to £20,000, going up to about £26,000 once you've got some experience. Senior executives will earn something in the region of £40,000 to £50,000.

DIRECT MAIL
Direct mail is so called because it comprises ads and promotional literature that go direct to the customer by post, fax or the Internet. Direct mail agencies perform the same functions as ad agencies, including account planning, creative work and production. They also organise getting the material out to potential customers. As ads become increasingly personalised, targeted direct mail is becoming a subject in its own right. It involves looking at consumer trends, database management, research and IT. Direct mail may also be done by a full service agency.

THE ADVERTISING AGENCY
Work experience in an advertising agency can be a good way for prospective marketers to learn more about brands and consumer trends. Understanding how an agency works will be useful when you are using them as a supplier.
Sean Harris, Managing Director of an advertising agency

in London: 'What we look for in work experience candidates is enthusiasm, a good personality and an interest in ads. If you want to contact an agency to see if they are taking anyone on, find out the name of the business director or human resources director and send them a letter.'

MARKETING – THE SPONSORED EVENT
What is your favourite part of the job?
One of the aspects of my job is that I work closely with the branding related to the sponsorship of a major sporting event in the UK.

Why did you decide on this job?
I got into this job because I'm a sport nut and I thought it would combine my interest in marketing with my interest in sport. And it did. Even though the event is only once a year, there's a lot to be done throughout the year.

What frustrates you about your job?
There are so many branding issues relating to the merchandise and promotional material. We are the main sponsor, but other companies have smaller sponsorship roles, i.e., they pay less money to have their name associated with the event. This leads to a set of interminable meetings with the event organisers about brand positioning on the merchandise. Everybody wants to get as much publicity as they can. The wrangling can get a bit boring. Last year all the t-shirts had to be reprinted as one of the other sponsors had managed to get their logo on to the front of the t-shirt when we think of that as where the main sponsor's logo should be. It might sound a bit petty, but you have to fight for your brand as the other marketing teams are out there putting pressure on the event organisers.

What else do you have to do in terms of sponsorship and the brand?
Each year we also have to think of new ways to involve our products in the event itself. We have to be creative and come up with ideas that will make people leave the event and not only remember our product name but make a connection with why we sponsor the event and what the value of our product is.

Branding at the event is also a key issue. The marketing team make sure the event is putting our logo in the best places for the TV coverage. For example, when a sports person is interviewed we ensure the brand is easy to see behind him or her.

It's a lot of work, and you can feel panicked, if we make mistakes it costs the company mega bucks. Sponsorship is a form of paid advertising. On the other hand when it all comes together and I'm at the event, I feel like part of a huge team and I love it!

Sarah Mills, 35, works for a multinational company that sponsors a national sporting event

MARKETING – THE ASSISTANT BRAND MANAGER
What do you like about your job?
I like the variety and the travel. We've got offices in Asia, New York and Edinburgh and I get to move about a lot. I've had a lot to do with the setting up of the New York office in terms of marketing and that's been exciting. It's perfect for this time of my life. In the past year I have been regularly travelling between New York and London, living between the two cities. I also get on with my boss, which is very important as we work so closely together.

How did you get your job?
I've always loved travelling. When I took a gap year in

Australia and Asia before university I knew I wanted a 'global' job that meant I could move around. When I decided to go into marketing I was thinking more of a big international 'milk round' firm, but quite by chance, when I finished my French degree, a friend of mine let me know about a junior job in the marketing department of my current firm. He made an introduction, I went to the interview and I got the job.

What frustrates you about your job?
Sometimes I feel a bit like a brand policeman and sometimes I feel like I'm knocking my head against a brick wall. When we set up the New York office we re-branded the company. This meant changing all of our headed notepaper and using new logos on all company material. In our Asian office some staff just refused to throw away the old paper because they thought it was wasteful. That meant they were still using the old paper even after the company had been re-branded. So a ludicrous situation ensued where I was trying to catch people out for misuse of paper. The real frustration was they didn't buy into the idea of the importance of company image and a consistent brand.

Simon Clarke, 22, Assistant Brand Manager at an international law firm in Edinburgh

CHAPTER 4

What You Could Be in PR

Public relations is all about building awareness and maintaining a long-term understanding between an organisation and its public.

There are usually three or four levels in a PR department. A junior is likely to be called something like a public relations executive, then the next level could be called a consultant, while the more senior level has more of a management function and could be called an account manager. The level above that is likely to be in charge of the whole PR function and could possibly be under a fifth level like a director. Responsibilities will differ, depending on the organisation, but the following are examples of the types of task you may do at different levels.

PUBLIC RELATIONS EXECUTIVE

The job could include answering simple media enquiries, performing administrative tasks such as updating contacts lists, writing press releases (edited and overseen by a manager), administrative tasks related to launches and events, organising photo shoots, keeping up to date with the press and compiling daily notes on the media, sending out press releases and other information, helping out at launches and events, writing articles and material for internal communications.

PUBLIC RELATIONS CONSULTANT

Similar to a public relations executive but with more responsibility, the public relations consultant is likely to deal face to face with clients, handle budgets and have a more hands-on approach when dealing with the media. He or she will be able to deal with crisis management, with reference to the manager, and will be required to give presentations to prospective clients.

PUBLIC RELATIONS MANAGER

A public relations manager has much more responsibility, will have people management skills, and will be responsible for a significant budget. In charge of producing PR strategy, he or she will be responsible for all elements of the PR mix, from crisis management to proactive media relations, and will be accountable for the team's results.

HEAD OF PUBLIC RELATIONS

This is a more senior role again, with greater accountability and responsibility. The head of public relations is responsible for overall PR strategy and must see that each account falls in with the larger picture. He or she handles the overall budget and deals with human resource issues and team motivation. This is a demanding role for which management skills, creativity and attention detail focus are all necessary.

DIRECTOR OF COMMUNICATIONS

This role will sometimes be at the head of the public relations and marketing departments. The director of communications is likely to be on the board and reporting to the CEO, and accountable for the success of communication strategies for the business. This is a high-profile management role that requires experience and drive.

PR AREAS

You can choose to work in house or in an agency. There are arguments for and against both: it really depends on what suits you. Generally, agencies offer a really good training ground, as you will work on a range of accounts. The downside of this is that you have more than one client and each one thinks they are the most important. If you work in house you have just one client, the company you are working for, so the relationship is more focused. Some people who make the move to in-house work from agency say the hours are better in house; but that will depend on the job.

Public relations is usually broken down into sectors and many people will eventually become specialists in one or more sectors. Examples are:

- financial

- healthcare

- telecommunications

- IT

- arts

- entertainment

- food and drink

- energy

- fashion

- public

- charities.

There is also a range of specialities within public relations. In many cases you will be asked to provide all of these functions, but sometimes, especially in larger companies, employees may have responsibility for different functions. These specialisations include:

- media relations

- crisis management

- public affairs – dealing with government

- internal communications – communications within the company

- corporate social responsibility

- event management

- financial/Investor relations.

THE SPECIALIST IN CRISIS MANAGEMENT

Crisis management can mean anything from dealing with a major air crash to dealing with a food scare or really any news that is likely to be damaging to a company's reputation.

I think it's the most exciting part of communications because there is a huge amount of pressure to get it right and handle it properly. Because there is so much adrenaline flowing, sometimes people get over-excited and they say the wrong thing just because they feel they should say something.

For example, any major transport incident becomes a crime scene, and the only people who should tell the press vital information like the number of dead or injured are the police. When crisis situations are handled badly, the PR people start confirming speculation. Good crisis management is about taking some of the panic out of it. It's all about putting processes in place that mean you are prepared for any eventuality.

An instance of that is that when Princess Di died, Mercedes pulled their ads as she had died in a Mercedes. They are likely to have had a system in place that meant that the ads were pulled as soon as the story came out.

If you're an airline you have to have excellent systems in place. If there is an air crash you need to have a holding statement always prepared, something to say to the press while the facts are ascertained. Then the company can react to the facts in a considered way.

While something like a crash is always an awful situation and disastrous for those involved, it is still possible to minimise the negative impact on the company. As long as you manage and deal with it in a structured and honest manner the company can at least emerge from the tragedy having been open.

It is vital when a major incident happens that the public is addressed by a senior member of the organisation. It's as much about the message as it is about the messenger. When people see the title 'Communications Director' or whatever they immediately think 'spin doctor'.

Anyone interested in this area should think about working in public relations for an airline. They probably have the most sophisticated systems in place for crisis management. Also, as international organisations, airlines must think of global and local solutions to crisis management communications.

Charles Gordon, 30, freelance Public Relations Consultant
and expert in crisis management
London

THE HEALTHCARE EXPERT
What do you see as the value of your job?
What excites me is the opportunity to really change things for the better. Especially in health, giving people the right kind of information can help them live healthier/better lives. You can also bring government policy to life – make it real for people.

Is it a good job to have if you have a family?
Yes, I think it is nowadays. Agency culture has changed completely. At the end of the day employers understand the value of good people and they are increasingly likely to be

more flexible and aware of employees' family commitments.

What advice would you give to someone starting out?
Qualifications are important. I would say seek out the right courses and the right degree. In my view being good at writing is one of the key skills for successful PR and that's something a lot of new recruits seem unaware of. In the end you are a backroom person – a facilitator. I wouldn't advise anyone to go into PR if they want to be in the limelight – that's what you do for others.

Claire Cater, Expert in Healthcare Communications,
Brighton

THE PR NEWS HOOK

PR departments will try and hook their products and messages into the news. For example, a good way to build brand messages through PR is to be seen as an expert in your business sector. A mortgage company might send out press releases with figures and comments each time interest rates change. That way a journalist using the figures and comments will give the mortgage company a mention. Readers will read the article and perceive the mortgage company as an expert in the sector – free coverage.

Similarly, a PR department might send out a press release that could be turned into a feature. For example, just before the May bank holiday, a DIY firm might send out a press release listing the five most common DIY disasters that happen on bank holidays, with advice on how to avoid them. The Homes and Property section of a paper has a fun story to run with a news hook (a specific timely event that makes a story newsworthy), and the DIY company gets a mention and is positioned as an expert.

WHAT THE JOURNALIST SAYS

'Sometimes it feels as if PR people don't have a clue what we are up against. I work on a national tabloid and contribute to a weekly financial section. We need to know when the best products come out on the market and need to get comment from the big financial institutions and organisations when we're writing stories. I know who the good PRs are in the sector. They are the ones who don't hassle you with waste-of-time non-stories on the day you have to file and who know that when you ask for information that's when you need it. It drives you mad if you've got a big story to write and are collecting information from a range of companies. You can end up having to chase up about six people for the information. Our deadlines are serious – there's no way we can miss one – so if I ask for a quote by the end of the day that's when I need it. We don't get a second chance and we won't give you one.

I would say to anyone going into PR: be selective with what you send journalists. You lose credibility if you send us puff. Only use the phone when absolutely necessary, otherwise use e-mail. It is infuriating when you are trying to concentrate on a story and PR companies repeatedly call you with useless information. Also, know your area really well and journalists will take you much more seriously. As a financial journalist I know my sector like the back of my hand and therefore don't have time for financial PR people who don't have a clue about finance.'

Paul Gibson, 44, Financial Journalist
London

THE ACCOUNT EXECUTIVE
Why are you in PR?

I work in a big PR agency in central London. I've always been fascinated by current affairs, particularly business news. When we get a story in a big paper or on the

broadcast news it feels brilliant. The job is very buzzy. Lots
to do. We're in contact with loads of agents and celebrities.
But it's really hard work and you've got to be able to deal
with loads of stress. Some of the accounts here I love, but
others are less interesting. Your day-to-day life at work
depends very much on your client. Their expectations can
be out of step with reality. A new type of biscuit is not going
to make the front page of the *Sun*, but sometimes you get
the impression that's what the client expects!

Martin Russell, 24, Account Executive for a PR agency,
London.

PR PRINCESSES

The unofficial princesses of London celeb parties are Fran
Cutler and Meg Matthews (the former Mrs Noel Gallagher).
With a contact list to die for, they can turn any bar or club
into *the* cool place just by inviting a few of their mates
along, who as we all know include the likes of Kate Moss
and Jude Law. Sounds good, spending your life at parties.
But you can bet your life there's some hard graft involved.
Part of what makes Meg and Fran so good at what they do
is their incredible contacts. In fact, collecting contacts over
your career is key to all PR jobs. From your first job
onwards, maintain good relationships with people you meet
through your work. Hoard phone numbers, remember
names and build up your own contact list. This should
include journalists, celebrity agents or anyone in the
business who is excellent at their job. By the time you are
at the middle stage of your career, the quality of your
contact list, particularly journalists who write about your
sector, is likely to be a major factor in any interview.

HOW DO PR AGENCIES WORK?

There are literally hundreds of PR agencies in the UK. Some specialise in one sector, while others offer an 'across the board' service. The size of agencies varies enormously. Big agencies like Weber Shandwick, for example, are vast international companies with offices and affiliations round the world, while others may have set up with nothing more than a couple of consultants and a couple of computers in the front room.

PR agencies are taken on a retainer or short-term basis. It is a highly competitive business and another agency will take your business if you are seen not to perform to the highest of standards.

BAD DAY AT THE OFFICE?
I hate it when . . .
A bad day in PR can be horrific. You've got to be thick-skinned. Journalists often have a very negative impression of PR people. A pressurised journalist with a deadline can go off the handle if you can't get some information they need for an article. Your job is to try and give them everything they need. They can be as rude to you as they like and you just have to take it because you can't risk pissing one of them off. Often I'll be asked to sell-in a new press release (where you call up journalists and ask if they have got the release and try and tell them more about it). Unless you are speaking to your contacts within the media this can result in an entire day of abuse. It's sometimes the more junior staff who are given this task. You have to have a fantastic sense of humour and sense of the ridiculous to take it on the chin. The other thing that people don't realise is that sometimes the really difficult nutters will be put through to the press office. Occasionally, you can have days when people shout out at you all day. Plus you've got stressful deadlines of your own to stick to. However, these days are in the minority but it's essential anyone thinking about this job considers it. If you're not the sort of person who can bite their tongue and take things with a pinch of salt, then it might not be the right job for you.

On the good side, it's brilliantly varied, very team-orientated, creative and fun. I've got to be organised otherwise all the work gets on top of me but I find it really stimulating. My favourite part of the job is overseeing events. It's just great when everything comes together and all my ideas have turned into a successful event that has been enjoyed by the company and our clients.

Janey Simmons, 26, PR Executive for a financial services company, Leeds

THE JOB WASN'T ME

When I left university I worked for a year as a graduate trainee at a big PR agency in central London. I found the experience surreal. The main account I worked on was for a company that made toilets. The work seemed shallow and meaningless to me. I couldn't believe I had spent all that time at university to end up in a job that promoted toilets. Everyone else at the agency seemed totally into it and no one seemed to see it as a pointless waste of time. I got really depressed and realised I had made a totally wrong career choice. I was expected to sometimes spend my free time at awful parties with men in suits talking about toilet sales. It soon became clear to myself and the PR company that it wasn't for me. I realised I am not particularly sociable and that was an important part of the job. Also an innate enthusiasm is important as your job is to get excited about what you are promoting. I thought about moving to an agency with charity accounts or something I could believe in a bit more. But I realised that I did not enjoy socialising in a work context. Subsequently I went back to university and pursued a career in academia that suits me much better.

Matthew Stevens, 32, ex-PR trainee, Hampshire

CHAPTER 5

How do I get into Marketing and PR?

WHILE YOU'RE STUDYING

If you are studying or have just left school, start thinking *now* about where you want to get to. The Association of Graduate Recruiters (AGR) suggests you should be thinking about your career at least by your first year at university. (Having said that, lots of successful people don't get themselves together until long after that, so don't worry: it's never too late to be who you could have been!) You should be thinking about your CV and how you are going to make yourself attractive to employers. Here are a few ideas:

- do some marketing-/PR-related work experience in the holidays

- get some sales experience

- find a club in which you can learn key skills like teamwork or leadership

- since you want to be involved in marketing communications, why not find something to promote? It could be a college society or newspaper, or a student-run club night.

- get involved in an aspect of student media such as college radio or the college paper

- if there is an issue you feel strongly about, why not start a society or website to promote your ideas?

- get some commercial sales experience so you have an understanding of sales targets.

WORK EXPERIENCE – MAKE IT COUNT
Advice from Liz Rhodes MBE, Director of the National Council for Work Experience.

'These days work experience is more important than ever. Some employers won't look at CVs without evidence of work experience. A recent survey indicated that it is one of the most successful ways of getting a permanent job. Work experience is a broad term covering everything from part-time voluntary work to a full-time placement at an organisation. It can be a very productive period. We suggest that for it to work well the employer must think carefully what the individual will be doing and provide some kind of support.

'The student ought to be inducted, preparing them for going into the organisation. Equally, it is important that the student starts out by thinking what they want to achieve and reflects on what they have achieved. After all, the point of work experience is to learn skills that would be valuable to an employer and to help individuals identify what makes them a useful member of staff. In interviews it is crucial that a person is able to talk about what they have to offer. We also suggest that some form of payment is made during work experience.'

VOLUNTARY WORK

Voluntary work can give your career a kick-start. For those wanting to work in the charity sector this is a must. However, doing voluntary work for a charity can offer the opportunity to gather useful work skills, even if you have your eyes on a job in the commercial sector. Andie Lamb, Director of Reprieve – a charity that works to assist prisoners facing execution in America and the Caribbean – says volunteers for her organisation can gain valuable PR experience. 'As a small charity, volunteers are crucial to our survival. The potential is there for volunteers to gain invaluable PR experience. One of the tasks our volunteers are likely to get involved in is publicity generation for cases that we are assisting. Because we are small, volunteers may end up getting experience they wouldn't get in a larger organisation. It's all hands on deck here! So volunteering is not just helping a good cause. All the work done for us can go down on a volunteer's CV and works towards their personal career development.'

In most cases there will be a selection process involved in finding work as a volunteer. Volunteer opportunities exist around the world and can be an excellent way of combining an interest with developing your career potential. Go to www.gap-year.com for more information on volunteer opportunities abroad.

THE GRADUATE ROUTE

You are likely to need a degree in some discipline to get into marketing and PR, unless you have worked up through a company's ranks (though often a degree is necessary for this entry route as well). Increasingly, graduates are recruited by large organisations and taken on to their marketing traineeships. Getting a place on one of these schemes is highly competitive. To find out more on graduate traineeships go to the graduate recruitment website at www.prospects.ac.uk and search their job section. Also, speak to your university careers advisor.

For entry into a degree course in any subject, the usual minimum requirement is two or three A-levels and at least two or three GCSEs (grades A to C) in other subjects. If you don't have those qualifications, don't worry: entry requirements do vary between institutions. Other qualifications such as vocational A-levels (Advanced GNVQs) and Edexcel (BTEC) National Diplomas are usually accepted instead of A-levels.

Although specific marketing and PR qualifications are not essential, they do give you an advantage in a highly competitive area. For example, there are universities and colleges that offer an HND with market research. You could also look at degrees in marketing or business studies with marketing modules. When searching for a course, always look at the modules over the course. Plan carefully which modules you take and keep your focus on the end result.

A few universities and colleges now offer degrees in public relations. For PR, a business studies degree with communications modules is likely to be just as useful.

Degrees taken by graduates working in marketing

Degree subject	Percentage of graduates
Business Studies	34.0
Modern Languages	13.5
History	9.5
Psychology	8.0
Geography	7.0
Law	4.0
Biology	4.0
Economics	4.0
Chemistry	2.5
Maths	2.5
Physics	1.0

Source: Hobson's Graduate Career Directory 2001/workthing.com

THE NON-GRADUATE ROUTE

There are some opportunities for non-graduates. Some organisations will take employees without degrees, but who have A-levels (or equivalent), work experience and vocational qualifications. If you don't have a degree and don't feel you have the time to do one, get as many industry-specific qualifications as you can and start to build up your work experience.

PROFESSIONAL/VOCATIONAL QUALIFICATIONS

PR

The Institute of Public Relations (IPR) runs its own courses, available to people with no experience in PR, and offers career development qualifications in the form of their Advanced Certificate and Diploma. Many of these courses are part-time and can be taken while working. The IPR also offers distance learning. Go to their excellent website (www.ipr.org.uk) for more information on these courses and on day workshops. A journalism qualification can also be extremely useful for PR because it teaches you to write in a journalistic style (key for writing press releases) and helps you to get into the head of a journalist.

The IPR has approved the following PR-related courses:

Institution	Qualification(s)	Course length	Contact info.
Bournemouth University	BA (Hons) in PR MA in corporate communication	4 years; year 3 spent on placement 1 year full-time or 2 years part-time	www.bournemouth. media. ac.uk
Cardiff University (Centre for Journalism Studies)	Postgraduate Diploma in Public and Media Relations	2 terms full-time plus 200 hours work placement	www.cf.ac.uk

Institution	Qualification(s)	Course length	Contact info.
University of Central England in Birmingham	BA (Hons) in Media and Communication (Public Relations)		www.media courses.com
University of Central Lancashire, Lancashire Business School (Department of Journalism)	BA (Hons) in PR/ PR and Marketing/ PR and Management	3 years full-time or 4 years sandwich (includes a 48- week placement)	www.uclan.ac.uk
Dublin Institute of Technology	MA/Postgraduate Diploma in Public Relations	1 year; 2–4 weeks spent on place- ment after finals	www.dit.ie
Institute of Public Relations	Diploma/Advanced Certificate in PR		www.ipr.org.uk
University of Leeds (Trinity and All Saints University College)	BA (Hons) in Media with Management MA/Postgraduate Diploma in Public Communication		www.tasc.ac.uk
Leeds Metropolitan University	BA (Hons) in PR/ PR with Language MA in European PR	3 years, or 4 years including 1 year work placement	www.lmu.ac.uk
University of Lincoln	BA single and joint honours in PR	3 years, or 4 years including 1 year work placement	www.lincoln.ac.uk
London Metro- politan University (London City Campus)	MA in Media Management (PR)	1 year full-time/ 2 years part-time	www.london met.ac.uk

Institution	Qualification(s)	Course length	Contact info.
Manchester Metro-politan University	MA in PR	1 year with placement	www.mmu.ac.uk
PRISA Education and Training Centre	PRISA Higher Certificate PRISA	2 years 1 year	PO Box 31749, Braamfontein, South Africa
Queen Margaret University College, Edinburgh	BA (Hons) in Corporate Communications	4 years with optional placement	www.qmuc.ac.uk
College of St Mark and St John, Plymouth	BA (Hons) in PR	3 years; 4 weeks at end of year 2 spent on placement	www.marjon.ac.uk
University of Stirling (Film and Media Department)	MSc in PR	1 year (voluntary placement during March); 3 years by distance learning	www.fms.stir.ac.uk
Thames Valley University	MSc in Corporate Communication	1 year full-time/ 2 years part-time	www.tvu.ac.uk
University of Ulster	BSc (Hons) in Communication, Advertising and Marketing		www.ulst.ac.uk
West Hertfordshire College (Watford Campus)	PRCA Diploma in International PR	1 year post-graduate course with placement during May	www.westherts. ac.uk

WHY TRAINING IS INVALUABLE
Training addresses both the essential skills for marketers and then also the 'edge' skills (emerging practices, provoking ideas and thinking differently). (Source: CIM)

MARKETING

There are over 1,500 marketing-related degree courses in the UK. Some of these are single honours, while others combine marketing with a relevant subject such as accounting, a language or computer science. Go to www.ucas.com and do a search for marketing degrees to find one in your area.

The largest marketing body in the UK, the Chartered Institute of Marketing (CIM), offers the largest range of professional qualifications in marketing. Many of the courses are part-time and can be taken while working. In some cases companies will pay for employees to do this kind of training. There are four levels of study:

● Foundation – an introduction to marketing as an essential business discipline. Good for those starting out and for career changers, as this course is for people with little or no experience in marketing. You must be over 18 to do this course.

● Certificate – if you haven't done the Foundation course, to do the CIM's Certificate in Marketing you will need to be over 18 with two A-levels or equivalent, or over 20 with one year's full time sales or marketing experience.

● Advanced Certificate - you will need the CIM's Certificate in Marketing, or a non-marketing degree from a CIM-approved university, or HNC/HNDs or NVQ/SVQs Level 3.

● Postgraduate Diploma in Marketing – you should have either the Advanced Certificate or a degree/postgraduate qualification containing a substantial amount of marketing modules or equivalent qualification.

Communication Advertising and Marketing Foundation (CAM) qualifications:

- Advanced Diploma in Communication Studies

- Higher Diploma in Public Relations

- Higher Diploma in Integrated Marketing Communications.

Chartered Institute of Marketing (CIM) Qualifications:

- Introductory Certificate in Marketing

- Certificate in Marketing

- Certificate in Marketing (residential training)

- Certificate in Marketing (online, blended e-learning)

- HMA Certificate in Marketing (residential in-company tailored training)

- Postgraduate Diploma in Marketing

- Advanced Certificate in Marketing

- Advanced Certificate in Marketing (residential training route)

- Advanced Certificate in Marketing (online, blended e-learning)

- Advanced Certificate in Arts Marketing

- Postgraduate Diploma in Marketing

- Intensive Diploma in Marketing (residential training route)

- e-Marketing Award

- CRM Development Award.

Institute of Professional Sales (IPS) qualifications:

● Certificate in Professional Sales (online, blended e-learning)

● Advanced Certificate in Professional Sales Management (residential training route)

● Advanced Certificate in Professional Key Account Management (residential training route)

● Intensive Diploma in Professional Sales (residential training course).

PAYING FOR QUALIFICATIONS

The best-case scenario is to get a traineeship in a company in which the bill for your training will be picked up the company. However, any cash you invest in your own training is unlikely to be wasted, and employers will be impressed if you have taken your career development into your own hands. Paying for your own professional qualifications does show commitment to the cause! But most of us find it hard enough to make ends meet, without having to find more money to pay for expensive courses. If you are already working for a company, and you are not happy with the level of training you are receiving, find a training package that is directly relevant to your job and see if your company has the budget to put you on the course.

If all else fails, it might be worth taking out a Career Development Loan. Think carefully before you do this, however, and always consider what debts you are already paying back. Draw up a financial plan: look at your monthly expenditure and your monthly income. If you think you have the spare cash to repay a loan, always leave yourself a margin – just to be sure you can cover the payments.

HOW TO GET A CAREER DEVELOPMENT LOAN

You can get a Career Development Loan of between £300 and £8,000. The DfES pays the interest while you learn. The loan will pay up to 80% of your course fees unless you have been out of work for three months or longer, in which case you may be able to get 100% of your course fees. It will also pay for your books, travel, childcare and any other direct expenses that are related to your course. When your course is finished you pay the loan back to the bank over an agreed period at a fixed rate of interest. You can get a Career Development Loan though three high street banks: Barclay's, the Co-operative and Royal Bank of Scotland. Go to www.lifelonglearning.co.uk for more information, and look at www.support4learning.org.uk.

CHOOSING A COURSE - CHECK LIST

Before you choose a course, ask the following key questions:

● Do I have the time to attend and study for the course?

● How is this course going to help with my career?

● Does it teach me everything I want to know? If not, is there another course that does?

● How much time will it take me to travel to the course?

● Does the course offer distance learning?

● Can I see myself completing the course?

● Have I read any of the course literature to see if it will sustain my interest?

● Can I afford it?

● Can I pay back any loans I'm taking out to pay for the course?

ROUTES INTO THE PUBLIC SECTOR

The government is one of the biggest PR employers in the UK. It also has a large marketing and new media department. There are some fantastic jobs available in PR, press, marketing, publicity and e-communications. Entry is at Assistant Information Officer level, posts go right up to Director of Communications, and you can work in government departments and agencies across the UK. The department that runs all government communications is the Government Information and Communications Service (GICS). You have to apply for a specific job, posted in the media section of the *Guardian*, or on the service's website, www.gics.gov.uk. If you are offered an interview you will be invited to an assessment centre where you will be interviewed and given a written test. This may all sound daunting, but once you're in, GICS offers excellent training. Jane Wood, Press Officer for a government department, says, 'After I graduated with an arts degree, I worked in newspapers before I got this job. Some days can be really hectic when I'm reacting to press calls. It is the civil service, so sometimes all the processes can get you down. On the other hand, some of the work is very interesting and you get paid overtime here and your job is secure – something totally unheard of in the media! Government jobs offer good employee rights like equal opportunities and maternity benefits.'

HOW TO BECOME A GRADUATE TRAINEE

A graduate traineeship offers a solid grounding in management and communications skills.

According to workthing.co.uk, among the most respected for marketing are the traineeships offered by companies dealing in FCMG (fast moving consumer goods) such as Unilever, Mars, and Procter and Gamble.

All companies offer different schemes. Go to their websites

to find out more. For example, Unilever takes on graduates once a year to work in marketing as part of its Unilever Companies Management Development Scheme. Starting salaries for marketing trainees are somewhere in the region of £23,000. You could start out in a position such as assistant brand manager but are likely to get a management appointment within two to three years. Most marketing related graduate training schemes will involve hand-on experience in brand management and product development.

If you are considering doing a graduate traineeship, then make your enquiries sooner rather than later. Although traineeships are likely to start in September, the selection process can take up to a year. Do your research, and look for a traineeship that offers you the kind of experience you need for your future career. Because traineeships offer such great experience they are highly competitive. But don't be put off. Even if you don't get the job, the experience of taking part in the selection process will be incredibly useful as it will give you first-hand experience of what kinds of questions you are likely to be asked at future/other interviews.

WHERE TO GET ADVICE

Graduates, undergraduates and sixth-formers will have a wealth of advice available from the careers advisory service in their schools and colleges. Careers advisors should be able to point you in the right direction for job opportunities and information in your area. As a graduate, even if you are no longer living in the city in which you studied, you may be entitled to careers advice at your local university. Call up the main graduate careers advisory service in your area to discover if you are eligible. If you are not a graduate, recent graduate or school leaver your local library or job centre may have just the answer. Most large libraries and job centres offer some kind of careers advisory service. This will normally involve an interview with a trained specialist, during which they will ascertain what you are looking for and probably refer you to books on careers in the library. It is likely that they will also send you some extra information on your chosen career.

Another route is to pay a private organisation to give you a career consultation, which is likely to include a psychometric test. These can cost anything up to £1,000 and sometimes you can get as good a service in the local library for nothing. There are free psychometric tests available on the Internet, so you could always do one of these first and see what you think.

The main thing to remember is that there is an enormous amount of advice and information out there. Make sure you get as much help as possible. The more research and thinking you do the easier you will find it at interview when you are asked why you have chosen a particular career path.

For general advice about marketing and PR careers you should check out the following websites:

● www.ipr.org.uk

● www.cim.co.uk

● www.occupationonline.gov.uk

● www.prospects.ac.uk

● www.workthing.co.uk

● www.monster.co.uk

Have a look at the website reviews on page 77 to see which sites offer the most accessible information.

SKILLS EMPLOYERS LOOK FOR

The Association of Graduate Recruiters (AGR) has researched what employers are looking for. This is what they discovered:

People skills:

● leadership – taking responsibility and getting things done

- team working – working well with colleagues and being able to listen

- interpersonal skills – being good with people from a wide range of backgrounds and able to put your ideas across easily.

Self-reliance skills:

- self-awareness – feeling confident about yourself and what you do

- resourcefulness – having drive, using your initiative and planning ahead

- networking skills – being good at linking up with other people so you can help each other.

General skills:

- problem-solving – being practical and quick-witted

- commitment – being dependable, trustworthy and putting everything into your work

- flexibility – being adaptable and willing to do lots of different kinds of work.

Specialist skills:

- IT skills – expert computer knowledge (you need basic IT skills for almost every job)

- technical skills – knowledge of real work areas, e.g. marketing and PR qualifications

- business understanding – knowing what makes companies tick.

Source: *If Only I'd Known: making the most of higher education – a guide for student and parents*, available from the AGR at www.agr.org.uk

CAREER CHANGE

Hate your job? Feel trapped, think you've made the wrong decision and that there is no way out? Well, don't. Changing career is not as difficult as you might think. It is an upheaval and it may take a little time but it can be done. What's more, many people make a career change. The idea of a job for life is a semi-redundant one these days. If you've been working for a few years you will have quite a few marketable skills under your belt. Much career literature is aimed at school leavers and recent graduates, so you can feel that you've missed the boat. But honestly you haven't. It can be done, as long as you've got a good few years left in your career before you retire.

Step One: Working out what you would like to do takes time. If you think marketing and PR might be for you, keep researching. Talking to people who work in marketing and PR will be a big help. Try to network through friends and family and find out what's out there. You may also like to go to a careers consultant or make an appointment at your local library for a free session of careers advice. Remember, it may be the case that you could stay in your current career and move sideways. Think of the possibilities in your career first. It could just be that you are unhappy with your organisation, job or the area in which you are working.

Step Two: Go back to the section on skills and core competencies for marketing and PR (pages 19–23). Work out exactly what experience you have in these areas. Make a chart and write down your transferable skills. For example, experience of managing projects or budgets is highly relevant. Be really positive when you do this. It is likely that you will have many skills you never even think about. For example, are you used to working under pressure? Do you have good computer skills? Write everything down and do this over a period of a few days so you can keep coming back to your list.

Step Three: Now you have a list of your own core competencies and skills. Work out how they fit with the skills required for marketing and PR. Are there any gaps? These are your learning areas. You will need to fill these gaps somehow. This can be done through training. The best thing to do is to find a course that fills as many of those gaps as possible. You can do this while you are working, so as not to disrupt your life too much.

Step Four: Are you ready to take the leap? When making a career change the most sensible thing to do is not to burn your bridges. You have to discover if you've made the right decision. Ideally the least violent change can be made if you can stay in an area in which you already have some knowledge. This is one of the great advantages of moving to marketing and PR for career changers. Because marketing and PR are used in practically every field, it is likely that you will be able to pinpoint a marketing and PR job in your area. If you have been working in scientific research, for example, it would be a good idea to approach a scientific organisation or company.

Step Five: You may have to take a large cut in salary while you are at the learning stage. As long as you can keep to your financial commitments this is worthwhile because you will be gaining invaluable on-the-job experience. Just like any new job it's important not to be afraid to ask questions. You will be there to learn. Once you are up to speed you will probably find that your previous experience will come in handy. Remember, a different angle is a great thing in business – you may add a whole new dimension to your department.

AGR (Association of Graduate Recruiters) and AGCAS (Association of Graduate Careers Advisory Services) have the following advice for mature graduates. They say, be positive about what you've got to offer, 'older graduates have the one thing that younger graduates dream of – *experience* – whether that's work or life'. Take a look at their ten top tips on how to increase your chances at interview.

TEN TOP TIPS FOR MATURE GRADUATES
1. Produce a concise CV that clearly outlines all your relevant experience. Try and match your experience to the job requirements, and be prepared to produce more than one CV. If you really want the position then fully research each employer. As a minimum, visit the employer's website.

2. If you get an interview you're halfway there, so be confident! Be prepared to take along evidence if asked for.

3. Use positive language in tailored applications and at interviews. As a starting point, never apologise for your age.

4. Use contacts from previous jobs/friends/family – create your own network. Remember, you have probably met more people in your lifetime than the average graduate.

5. Identify the skills you developed from your previous work, studies, and general life experience – e.g. teamwork, communication and adaptability.

6. Stress your ability to hit the ground running – you know all about working for a living.

7. Demonstrate your experience when making effective business decisions and give examples.

8. Highlight your time-management, organisation and self-motivational skills. You've just spent a number of years improving these.

9. Demonstrate your flexibility and experience of studying and working in mixed age environments.

10. Convey your reliability, loyalty and confidence to manage change.

Source: AGR and AGCAS

THE INTERVIEW

Think of yourself as a marketing proposition. You are the brand: what have you got that will put you above the competitors in the market place?

As a person you have a lot to offer. Qualifications are important, but you will bring a lot of yourself to any job you do. Work out what you're good at. The key to any interview is to read the job specification carefully. Work out what they are looking for and think of examples of how your skills fit.
If you're straight out of college, take examples from your life that could be transferred to a work situation. You may be the kind of

person who's great at selling ideas: do others follow when you
lead? You could be fantastic at diplomacy: are you the one who
gets everyone to pay the house bills without argument? Be positive
and know your strengths. Write out a list with your top five
characteristics and instances that illustrate them. For example:

- resourceful: good at finding solutions to problems in stressful
  situations

- organised: budgets personal finances carefully and successfully

- team player: in joint projects focused on success of group
  rather than individual glory

- leadership: organise weekly group sports sessions

- detail-focused: good at proofreading, picking out spelling
  mistakes and spotting errors.

PUT YOUR BEST FOOT FORWARD

Have you ever seen those makeover programmes in which people
are trying to sell their house? Getting a job can be a bit like that.
You don't have to lie about yourself, you just have to work out what
the buyer wants and highlight your good points.

A survey published in *The Times* in March 2003 found that an
incredible nine out of ten UK graduates are turned down for a job
because their CVs are full of grammar and spelling mistakes.
Many graduates also sent their CV to the wrong person and if they
got to interview appeared to have done little or no research into
the company they wanted a job in.

By checking for spelling mistakes and ensuring you are writing to
the right person you put yourself ahead of the pack. It really is
that easy.

We all get nervous before interviews. But the first step is to
prepare really well.

PREPARING FOR INTERVIEW

Don't forget the three Rs: research, research and – you've guessed it – research. Read up about the company and sector. You should understand the product and its competitors. Find out who their customers are and what the company market share is.

You should be buzzing with ideas at an interview. Get a folder and collect as much information as you can about the communications industry. Marketing and PR are everywhere: on your cereal packet, on TV, on posters on the street, on buses – anywhere there is a space someone will be trying to persuade you to buy something. The majority of campaigns are aimed at the under 35s, so your opinion really is relevant. What works for you and what doesn't? Think in terms of audience: if it doesn't appeal to you, maybe it's aimed at someone older or younger, or at the opposite sex.

Go to a few PR agencies' or marketing agencies' websites and look at what they do. Most agencies will provide case studies of their best campaigns. Most important of all, make sure you go the website of the company or agency with whom you are having an interview and know it like the back of your hand. However, if you've looked at other agencies' and companies' websites, you can impress your interviewer with some really in-depth knowledge of the industry.

There are a series of publications read by the marketing, PR and advertising industries. They will be available in your local library or careers centre. Have a good look at these. You can find out about current campaigns, awards, bigwigs and hotshots. They include:

● *Media Week*

● *Campaign*

● *Creative Review*

● *Marketing*

● *Marketing Week*

● *PR Week*

Being media-aware and knowing about popular culture is useful.

Marketing and PR use popular culture to sell. You need to be switched on to different sections of the media. Start another folder and collect information about how different people use the media. Is the Internet used mainly by young people or silver surfers? Which celebrities appeal to which sections of the population? What computer games are big? If you are a young person trying to break into marketing and PR you can put your youth to your advantage. Who are the current icons of your generation? What is edgy and underground? These are the type of trends that marketing and PR organisations like to catch a ride with. A classic example of this is the Levi's campaign in which a glove puppet became the star. The puppet originated in a cheap video made by a French DJ and had already gained street kudos before 'starring' in the Levi's commercial.

Knowing your newspapers and Internet news sources is also vital. Most people working in communications will get all the UK papers delivered to their offices every day. Get your head round the UK press. You should have a sense of the political bias of each paper and its readers. This is important so you know where ads and editorial coverage should be aimed. Generally the BBC News website at www.bbc.co.uk is a fantastic source for the latest news: use it to help you impress with your up-to-the-minute knowledge. Be aware that marketing and PR will also target local press if that suits the audience and demographic required by their campaign.

If you are going for a communications job in a particular sector, know the trade press. For example, if you are aiming to work in house for an insurance company, do an Internet search to find out the trade press titles for the insurance industry. In PR, for example, a lot of communications will be aimed at the trade press as well as the nationals and the local press.

HOW TO ANSWER THAT KILLER INTERVIEW QUESTION
'What are your weaknesses?' How to tackle the question and why recruiters ask it

'As always, be open and honest. We all have weaknesses. First of all, when asked the question it is never implied it is within a work environment, so it would be perfectly acceptable to answer in a modest and humorous way (this could be, e.g., "my weakness is cooking"). Once the question has been set in a work / professional context, it is advisable to turn the question and explain that what can be a negative characteristic in one context can be positive in another. The key thing is not to worry about admitting a weakness but to focus on the fact that you know about it and to talk about the steps you have taken to address it. For example, you might say that time management used to be a weakness, however you now ensure that you start each day with a "to do" list which you then prioritise and as a result you now have things totally under control. Remember, it is important to understand the role you are applying for and ensuring your set of skills are those needed to successfully fulfil that role.

'Another tip is to avoid saying that being a perfectionist is a weakness, as if you class this as a weakness, then the only way to tackle this is to stop doing perfect work, which is possibly not the best signal to be sending out to a prospective employer!

'Although the interviewer should not expect an entirely honest answer, this question can be useful for them to see how intuitively the candidate deduces the qualities that the company would most desire.'

Advice from monster.co.uk

According to the Monster Meter (November 2002), over half of the 2,211 job seekers polled at monster.co.uk state that enthusiasm and willingness to learn is the most important quality to convey in an interview.

While the UK results closely mirror the overall poll results of 14,427 European site users, which showed that 50% of Europeans rate enthusiasm and willingness to learn as the most important qualities to convey, these results contrast greatly with those of Denmark, Germany and Italy. In Denmark, only 33% of site users selected enthusiasm and willingness to learn as the most important qualities, while 34% of German users and 39% of Italian users chose this option.

Consultants at monster.com explain that interviewers have to tailor their interview strategy not just to a particular role or company, but also to a particular country. What works in the UK might not work in Germany and what works in Germany won't necessarily work in France. Pre-interview research and preparation is essential.

As a rule of thumb, the interviewer is looking for three things:

● Can they do the job? (Ability)

● Will they do the job? (Motivation)

● Will they fit in? (Personality)

TEN TOP TIPS ON HOW TO SUCCEED IN A JOB INTERVIEW

1. Be prepared. Spare at least an hour or two to think about the job you've applied for, the firm it's part of and the field/industry, what questions you may be asked (your skills and experience) and what questions you may want to ask. Also prepare practical things like what you will be wearing, spare copies of your CV to bring with you and check the commuting route in advance (don't be late, it shows lack of respect and lack of interest!).

2. Give yourself space. Don't be rushed when answering a question, and take a deep breath if you lose balance. It's fine to ask for clarification and it's good to invest a bit of time with warm human narrative and establishing rapport. Speak slower rather than faster and pitch your voice lower rather than higher.

3. Show enthusiasm. Think about what motivates you about the job – will this job get you out of bed in the morning? The answer should be yes. And if that is the case, don't be afraid to show your enthusiasm.

4. You are a brand. If you have prepared a great application form you will have created an image in the minds of the recruiters. Think about that image and try to live up to or exceed it when you actually meet them. Be yourself – they will want to find out who you really are and how you will react to working conditions, so think about which of your personal traits will help you excel in this job and make sure you explain them with examples.

5. Present ideas. Well-considered opinions are respected, even by people who don't agree with everything you say.

6. Give and take. Let the interviewer discover your qualities according to their own mindset. Don't try to hog the conversation, avoid being brash and boastful, and prepare for trick questions with modest and humorous answers (e.g. what is the worst mistake of your career and what is your biggest weakness?).

7. Be honest. Potential employers want honest answers; don't be afraid to say that you're not sure or that you don't know.

8. Have a direction-focused approach when asking questions. Don't just mindlessly write huge lists of questions soliciting data about the company. A direction-focused approach means thinking about the context in which the company is located: how does it meet its challenges within its ambit and from rivals? What are its goals? Often an employer will ask you something like, 'Where do you see yourself in five years' time?' You might well want to ask the same of the company. Don't get too carried away with your own questions. Save some of your questions for a potential second interview.

9. Body language. Be friendly and smile. You should always look attentive - so do not slouch in your chair. Eye contact is very important, but make sure it looks natural. A smiling, relaxed face is very inviting. Having your hands resting casually in your lap rather than your arms folded across your chest is also more inviting. If you normally move your hands around a lot when you speak, tone it down. You don't want to look too

stiff, but you don't want to look like you're a bundle of
nervous energy.

10. Ask for time. You are a mature person with commitments
    and a life – don't be rushed into agreeing anything and
    make it clear that you are seeking an advantageous career
    move. Bear in mind that they may also want more time for
    assessments, personality tests, etc., or just for
    consideration. Also make sure what the next step is (when
    will they contact you / another interview?) when you leave.

Source: monster.co.uk

STOP AND THINK

So are marketing and PR really for you? If you think they might be,
the first thing to do is to get some work experience. Remember
that the key skills you use in marketing and PR are transferable
within different sectors and therefore there is massive scope if you
decide to pursue a career in marketing or PR or both.

Within marketing, particularly, the discipline offers a wide range of
job types. You could end up as a brand manager, a marketing
manager or a market research executive.

Think of the scope of marketing and PR when you do your work
experience. If you get your first job in a firm that sells cheese and
mayonnaise, the environment will be a different one from a TV
company. So try and get as much work experience as possible in
as many varied jobs as possible.

This book should have helped you to consider whether marketing
and PR would suit you. When embarking on any possible career
it's always wise to ask yourself:

● What is the value of the job?

● Does that fit in with my personal values?

● What parts of the job can I get excited about?

- Can I see a career progression for myself?

- What personal skills do I bring to this job?

Then, if you decide it is for you:

- In what areas do I need training?

- How do I go about getting work experience?

- How can I optimise my CV to make my skills fit?

If you are interested in marketing and PR but are not quite sure they are for you, you could also look at journalism, advertising, sales, publishing, graphic design and web design, any of which might be more suitable. The key is to feel excited by your career. If the information in this book doesn't get you going, then think of another career – after all, it's what you'll have to spend most of your life doing, so you should love it.

CHAPTER 6

Find Out More

BEST WEB SOURCES

The mother of all media websites is the *Guardian*'s fantastic media section on the award-winning *Guardian* website, www.guardian.co.uk. Updated daily, the media section has everything you need to know about the UK media. It's like a cheat sheet for anyone interested in the media. They take the best stories from the trade press (e.g. *Campaign*), giving you the latest news in marketing and PR, and follow all the media news stories and the latest trends in communications. Before any interview you should spend a few hours on the *Guardian* site. Extremely accessible and interesting, the media section is also a good starting point for job searches.

The Institute of Public Relations at www.ipr.org.uk and the Chartered Institute of Marketing at www.cim.co.uk offer the best information in terms of qualifications and specific development. The CIM website is packed with really useful marketing trend information. For the untrained marketer, however, the jargon can sometimes be a little confusing.

Workthing, Monster and www.careers-portal.co.uk are great for trends and also insights into working in marketing and PR. Both

feature excellent case studies and regular articles from marketing
and PR practitioners.

BEST NEWSPAPERS AND PERIODICALS

- The *Guardian* (Monday)

- *The Times* (Tuesday)

- *Media Week*

- *Campaign*

- *PR Week*

- *Creative Review*

- *Marketing*

- *Marketing Week*

- *Revolution*

- *Wired*

- *New Media Age*

The Institute of Public Relations also prints *Profile* and the
Chartered Institute of Marketing publishes *Marketing Business*,
Marketing Success and the *Journal of Marketing Management*.

BEST PRINT SOURCES

There are literally hundreds of books and leaflets about
advertising and PR. You could start with dipping into one or two of
the following:

AGCAS (Association of Graduate Careers Advisory Services).
  Information books on marketing, including: *Marketing and
  Market Research*, *Advertising*, *Public Relations*, and *Direct*

Marketing and Sales and Purchasing.
All about Public Relations, McGraw Hill
Careers in Marketing, Advertising and Public Relations, Adela
   Stanley, Kogan Page.
Degree Course Offers, Trotman Publishing.
Everything you Need to Know About Marketing, Patrick Forsyth,
   Kogan Page
Hollis UK Press and PR Annual, Hollis Directories
How to Make it in Marketing and PR, Virgin Books
*Introduction to Marketing: A step-by-step guide to all the tools of
   marketing,* Geoff Lancaster and Paul Reynolds, Kogan Page.
*Market Research: A guide to planning, methodology and
   evaluation,* Paul Hague and Peter Jackson, Kogan Page.
Marketing Communications: An integrated approach, P.R. Smith,
   Kogan Page.
Marketing, Retailing and Sales Casebook, Hobson's.
Media Careers in Marketing and *Media Careers in Advertising,*
   Purple House.
Sponsorship and Funding Directory, Springboard Student Services,
   CRAC (published annually).
Students' Money Matters, Trotman.
Teach Yourself Public Relations, Hodder & Stoughton
*University and College Entrance (The Big Guide),*UCAS
Working in Marketing, Careers and Occupational Information
   Centre (COIC).

USEFUL ADDRESSES

Association of Graduate Careers and Advisory Service (AGCAS),
Crawford House, Precinct Centre, Manchester M13 9EP; and
Abford House, 15 Wilton Road, London SW1V 1NJ. Tel: 020 7828
7506. Website: www.agcas.csu.ac.uk

Association of Qualitative Research (AQR), Suite 14, Davey House,
31 St Neots Road, Eaton Ford, St Neots, Cambridgeshire. Tel:
01480 407 227.
Website: www.aqr.org.uk.

British Market Research Association, Devonshire House, 60
Goswell Road, London EC1M 7AD. Tel: 020 7566 3636.
Website: www.brma.org.uk.

Careers and Occupational Information Centre (COIC), PO Box 298a, Thames Ditton, Surrey KTZ OZS. Tel: 020 8957 5030. Website: www.dfee.gov.uk.

Chartered Institute of Marketing (CIM), Moor Hall, Cookham, Maidenhead, Berkshire SL6 9QH. Tel: 01628 427120. Website: www.cim.co.uk.

Regional offices: Chamber of Commerce House, 22 Great Victoria Street, Belfast BT2 7BJ. Tel: 028 9024 4113; Third Floor, 100 Wellington Street, Glasgow G2 6DH. Tel: 0141 221 7700.

City and Guilds of London Institute, 1 Giltspur Street, London EC1A 9DD. Tel: 020 7294 2468. Website: www.city-and-guilds.co.uk.

Communication, Advertising and Marketing Foundation (CAM), Moor Hall, Cookham, Maidenhead, Berkshire SL6 9HQ. Tel: 01628 427180. Website: www.camfoundation.co.uk.

Department for Education and Employment, Student Support, Mowden Hall, Staindrop Road, Darlington, County Durham DL3 9BG. Tel: 01325 392852. Website: www.dfee.gov.uk.

Direct Marketing Association, Haymarket House, 1 Oxendon Street, London SW1 YEE. Tel: 020 7321 2525. Website: www.dma.org.uk.

Edexcel Foundation (BTEC), Stuart House, Russell Square, London WC1B 5DN. Tel: 020 7393 4444. Website: www.edexcel.org.uk.

Institute of Direct Marketing, 1 Park Road, Teddington, Middlesex TW11 OAR. Tel: 020 8977 5705. Website: www.theidm.co.uk.

Institute of Export, Export House, Minerva Business Park, Lynch Wood, Peterborough PE2 6FT. Tel: 01733 404400. Website: www.export.org.uk.

Institute of Public Relations, The Old Trading House, 15 Northburgh Street, London EC1V OPR. Tel: 020 7253 5151. Website: www.ipr.org.uk.

Institute of Sales and Marketing Management, Romeland House Romeland Road, St Albans AL3 4ET. Tel: 01727 812500. Website: www.ismm.co.uk.

Institute of Sales Promotion, Arena House, 66–68 Pentonville Road, London N1 9HS. Tel: 020 7837 5340. Website: www.ismn.co.uk.

International Public Relations Association. Website: www.ipra.org

Market Research Society, 15 Northburgh Street, London EC1V OJR. Tel: 020 7490 4911. Website: www.mrs.org.uk.

National Union of Journalists, Headland House, 308 Gray's Inn Road, London WC1X 8DP. Tel: 020 7278 7916. Website: www.nuj.org.uk

Public Relations Consultants Association, Willow House, Willow Place, London SW1P 1JH. Tel: 020 7253 6026. Website: www.martex.co.uk/prca.

Qualifications and Curriculum Authority, 29 Bolton Street, London W1Y 7PD. Tel: 020 7509 5555. Website: www.qca.org.uk.

Scottish Public Relations Consultants Association, 62 The Shore, Leith, Edinburgh EH6 6RA. Tel: 0131 553 6000. Website: www.harrisoncowley.com.

Scottish Qualifications Authority, Hanover House, 24 Douglas Street, Glasgow G2 7NQ. Tel: 0141 248 7900. Website: www.sqa.org.uk.

Student Award Agency for Scotland, Gleyview House, 3 Redheughs Rigg, South Gyle, Edinburgh EH12 9HH. Tel: 0141 248 7900. Website: www.sqa.org.uk.

Universities and Colleges Admissions Service (UCAS), Rose Hill, New Barn Lane, Cheltenham, Gloucestershire GL52 3LZ. Tel: 01242 227788. Website: www.ucas.com.